THE
NEW AGE
ENTREPRENEURS

THE
NEW AGE
ENTREPRENEURS

RANDOM HOUSE INDIA

Published by Random House India in 2012

1

Copyright © HT Media Limited 2012

Random House Publishers India Private Limited
Windsor IT Park, 7th Floor, Tower-B,
A-1, Sector-125, Noida-201301 (UP)

Random House Group Limited
20 Vauxhall Bridge Road
London SW1V 2SA
United Kingdom

ISBN 978 81 8400 176 1

Typeset by InoSoft Systems, Noida

Printed and bound in India by Replika Press Private Limited

CONTENTS

FOREWORD

The New Age Entrepreneurs is the first book in the Mint Business series, published as a result of a unique partnership between Mint and Random House India. Every year, Mint and Random House India will collaborate to bring you business books spanning behind-the-news stories, business insights, economic and business history, or, simply stories of businessmen and businesses.

The New Age Entrepreneurs is also the result of a collaboration between the southern region office of the Confederation of Indian Industry, catalyzed by Sequoia Capital.

The four southern states aren't recognized for the hotbeds of entrepreneurship that they are. Over the years, entrepreneurs from these states—with the possible exception of software stars from Karnataka and infrastructure czars from Andhra Pradesh—have acquired the reputation for being conservative, unimaginative, and risk-averse.

Nothing could be farther than the truth.

From sweetmeats to software, entrepreneurs from the southern part of the country have launched new companies with significant success. Some of the businesses are old, yet, the very fact that million-dollar businesses can be built from such things as traditional South Indian sweets or poultry farming is unusual enough to merit their inclusion in this book.

The entrepreneurs were selected from a shortlist of a few hundred that was vetted by audit firm Grant Thornton by a panel comprising Ashwin Mahalingam, assistant professor, Indian Institute of Technology, Madras; C.K. Ranganathan, Chairman and Managing Director, CavinKare Pvt. Ltd; R. Ramraj, Senior Advisor, Sequoia Capital India Advisors Pvt. Ltd; Raja Ganapathy, Vice-President, Marketing, Sequoia; Mahadevan Narayanamoni, Partner-

Corporate Finance And Office Practice Leader-Hyderabad, Grant Thornton; Sridhar Venkatachari, Partner-Transaction Advisory Services And Office Practice Leader-Chennai, Grant Thornton; and R. Sukumar, Editor, Mint. The panel was assisted by Mary Stella, Director, Confederation of Indian Industry; and Akhila Ramesh, Deputy Director, Confederation of Indian Industry.

SUKUMAR RANGANATHAN
Editor, Mint

PREFACE

This is the fourth year in a row where CII has brought out a book on the general theme of innovation and entrepreneurship. When we started three years ago, our intentions were two-fold. First, we wanted to showcase entrepreneurial activity in Tamil Nadu to attract investors, incubators, and entrepreneurs to the state to strengthen the entrepreneurial eco-system. Second, we wanted to inspire prospective entrepreneurs by showcasing compelling stories of successful entrepreneurs. We brought out our first publication *Star Trek* with stories of 101 entrepreneurs.

The following year, we decided to focus on the innovations that fuel entrepreneurship. Entrepreneurship and innovation, though used synonymously, are widely different. Not all innovators who become entrepreneurs innovate radically. The process of innovation is, therefore, as worthy of mention as that of entrepreneurship. Furthermore, while mainstream innovators and inventions are often widely publicized, there are several innovators with wide and far-reaching social impact that emanate from rural areas, academic environments and small and medium industries that often pass by, unheard of. We decided to showcase 25 such innovations through our next publication *Breakthrough*. Once again we intended to inspire innovators with this book.

For ages, a debate has raged on about whether entrepreneurship can be taught. Though one school of thought holds that entrepreneurship can be broken down into discrete principles that can be inculcated into curriculum, others opine that entrepreneurship is based on an 'urge' that can often not be articulated, let alone taught. In truth, we believe that the answer lies somewhere in between. It is not Nature or Nurture. Successful entrepreneurs might well have seeds of creativity embedded in their DNA, but can also be guided on their path towards success. In short, successful entrepreneurs are not people who do different things but also who do things differently to carve out a niche for themselves.

With this objective, last year we brought out the *CII – Entrepreneurs Handbook*. A book, which attempted to be a reference that entrepreneurs can use. It is not and does not purport to be a comprehensive guide on how to become a successful entrepreneur. Each issue was taken up in this handbook to be dealt with in considerably greater detail by the experts and stalwarts with a belief that potential entrepreneurs could enhance their livelihood of success by familiarizing themselves with the content of this book, and the lifecycle of an entrepreneurial venture.

One step further, this year, CII SR Taskforce on Entrepreneurship and Innovation is bringing out a book on success formulae of entrepreneurship in collaboration with Mint portraying the success stories of entrepreneurs from the southern states who have created a niche for themselves both in terms of innovation and a proven track record. I am sure this book will be the Bible for the budding entrepreneurs who can learn a lot from their role models.

C.K. RANGANATHAN
*Chairman, CII SR Taskforce on Entrepreneurship & Innovation
and CMD, Cavin Kare Pvt. Ltd*

INTRODUCTION

The success gene: Does it exist?

As you read through this fabulous book, you are bound to be amazed at the diversity and variety of entrepreneurs covered here. Entrepreneurs who are diverse not merely because of the different sectors they represent but also because of the different paths they have chosen to success. For me, what stands out is the effort to distil the secret sauce behind each success story into a compelling insight that informs as much as it provokes thought.

In these couple of pages, I would like to focus the spotlight on a topic that has intrigued me a lot in my journey with entrepreneurs. What's common to successful entrepreneurs? Does an entrepreneur DNA exist? Is there a code that typifies the attitude and behaviour of path breaking entrepreneurs that, selfishly, would help us identify the next set of market leaders? At Sequoia Capital, we are privileged to have been early investors in more than 50 companies in India—some of which feature in this book—that today gives us a rich source of material to look for answers.

Single-minded focus and passion

Successful entrepreneurs bring a burning focus and passion to the business they are building. We notice that they rarely have personal interests and hobbies because they spend all their time, outside of family time, thinking and building their businesses. When entrepreneurs start having distractions, especially in the form of serious personal or business interests outside their main business, it is usually a 'red-flag' for us. It is easy to dismiss these driven individuals as 'quirky' because they may not be as well-rounded as the ideal VP-

Business Development we meet in large corporates; but this single-minded focus leads entrepreneurs to build great companies.

Tenacity

All young companies face challenges. Many of them reach 'dead ends' multiple times in their journey. We rarely see a company with a bar graph that does not depict this journey. The best entrepreneurs we know refuse to give up—they climb dead-end walls, create options out of nowhere, and find sources of succour for their companies to tide them through the bad times. It is important to highlight that this tenacity is best accompanied by the choice of the right market to demonstrate it in because there is not much value to be created when you operate in small or unprofitable markets.

'Customer service is not just a department'

This now-famous quote is from our well-known US portfolio company Zappos that was recently acquired by Amazon.com. Successful entrepreneurs bring a maniacal focus on the end-customer to their companies. Be it a B2B or a B2C business, this focus on the end-customer frequently helps separate winners from the also-rans, even in categories with seemingly low product differentiation.

Attracting and empowering talent

It cannot be a coincidence that the best entrepreneurs also attract the best management talent. These entrepreneurs learn very early that they cannot do it all by themselves and go about building teams that can help them execute their vision. Many of the entrepreneurs I know have, at different stages of their growth, struggled with empowering their management teams and have found it tough to let go of control, but have soon realized its virtues and gone on to create multiple leaders within the organization. Another important aspect of making their team feel empowered is to generously share the rewards of success as the business scales up. This allows the entrepreneur to create and distribute ownership of the company across the organization, and is the best way to incent teams.

Leadership
Being an entrepreneur is no lifestyle job. Many tough decisions have to be taken and being a leader is an essential characteristic of success. Having an unwavering focus on the end objective even as you navigate day-to-day vicissitudes calls for true leadership. Taking tough and unpopular decisions, especially in times of pain, requires the entrepreneur to feel lonely at times, and the successful ones have repeatedly demonstrated this ability. 'Feeling lonely', however, does not mean alienating the team; successful entrepreneurs are able to take the uncommon path and inspire people in that direction.

'Everything is not core'
Removing and deleting chaff takes tremendous thought and effort. Whether it is products, people, or markets—the best entrepreneurs bring a razor to their view on what is required for their business. Simple as it sounds, we have seen that the ability to remain lean and focused on what's core for a business usually separates the leader. The tough choice between thoughtfully sowing the seeds for the next stage of growth through investments versus a tactical move that can generate incremental revenue is the real test that differentiates the truly successful entrepreneurs from the not-so-successful ones.

While I have attempted to lay out six stand-out similarities among successful entrepreneurs we have partnered with, I must conclude by recognizing the innate individuality of every one of these founders. Each of these entrepreneurs has a unique story that stands out, and a unique set of qualities that deserve mention and respect. To create a successful business out of nothing requires creativity, innovation, and a desire to be different that makes them strong individuals who stand out in the crowd. I see this book as an ode to these successful individuals and hope that we see many more such wonderful success stories emerging from India in the future.

ABHAY PANDEY
Managing Director, Sequoia Capital

1

Accel Frontline Pvt. Ltd

In for the long haul
N.R. Panicker

ACCEL FRONTLINE PVT. LTD

Founder: N.R. Panicker

Year of founding: 1991

Headquarters: Chennai

Website: www.accelfrontline.in

Area of business: Information technology

Revenue: ₹330.81 crore in 2010–11

Profit: ₹6.34 crore in 2010–11

Uniqueness

*With a clear plan to boost profit margins by
tapping global clients—gained from strategic acquisitions—
for greater international business, Accel Frontline
may well make a credible run at its goal of
$500 million revenue in five years.*

By Vidya Padmanabhan

In recent months, information technology entrepreneur N.R. Panicker has been a part-time farmer, travelling every two weeks to visit his plantation in the village where he grew up—Pattanakkad in Kerala—to tend to his coconut trees and fish farms.

The newfound interest in his father's vocation, which he had left behind to start an IT career, doesn't mean the 57-year-old is on cruise mode after two decades at the helm of Accel Frontline Ltd, the company he founded in Chennai in 1991.

In fact, he is only getting his second wind to power Accel off the plateau it has hit in the past decade.

In August 2011, Accel Ltd, Accel Frontline's holding company, bought out the 51 per cent stake of its joint venture partner BT Frontline—a unit of British Telecommunications Plc.—to re-emerge as the majority stakeholder after more than six years.

'The company direction is normally decided by the majority partners,' Panicker says. 'I was not able to pursue my dream of making it a big company. Naturally, they are very careful about the money they invest.'

With Accel now holding a 68 per cent stake, just as it did in 2001 before the first joint venture partner came in, Panicker is now free to pursue his plans for the company.

'We want to make it a $500 million company in five years,' he says. 'Everyone here is aware that this is the dream we are chasing.'

The entrepreneurial urge seized Panicker during an early stint with an IT company in Delhi, when he became a fan of the enterprising Punjabis he saw around him, he says.

But the seed was really sown when he was a child growing up in Kerala in the 1960s.

A bright student from an impoverished home without electricity, and going to a minimally equipped Malayalam-medium village school, he found innovative ways to enrich himself, visiting local tea stalls both to listen to the radio as an aspiring professional musician, and to listen to the heated political debates that were often a staple there.

For extra reading, he would head to the local Communist Party office, where he would read the only literature available there: journals from the former Soviet Union and East Germany. On the streets, he would often watch slogan-chanting, red flag-waving party workers march in rallies.

Even at that young age, the sceptic in him would think: 'What we really need are jobs.'

As he went on to an engineering college in Thiruvananthapuram—where a scholarship paid his fees and friends pooled money to help move him from a ₹10-a-month room in a lodge to the college hostel—another thought came to him: 'If you don't have money, nobody gives you any respect. How long can you be an underdog?'

It was his second job—as a customer service executive in Hindustan Computers Ltd (HCL) in Coimbatore and then in Chennai—that gave him the confidence and contacts needed to branch out on his own. By 1988, he was ready.

Well, almost. He quit his position as a senior manager for

customer support in charge of several regions to start a computer accessories business, in which he believed it was possible to earn large margins.

Panicker had the assurance of support from friends as he surrendered the amenities—phone, car—that he had enjoyed as an HCL manager. But he found his plans falling apart soon afterwards. A friend who had promised him a telephone—imperative for doing business in those pre-cellphone days—backtracked.

Sleep eluded Panicker for three nights after that. His daughter was five years old, his son three. He lived in a rented house in Chennai and realized he didn't have enough cash for his business to survive for six months. He called Delhi and withdrew his resignation.

'But I wasn't calling off my plan,' he says. 'When you're confident you can get sufficient cash flows, only then should you jump into it.'

For the next two years, he saved and planned, and made the real jump in 1991 at the age of 36, this time to start a low-capital computer maintenance business and training school. (He still didn't have a telephone. In the beginning, his stationery displayed the number of a public phone booth downstairs.)

'My dream was to make it a ₹100-crore company in 10 years—and (I had) no capital,' he says, laughing. The total capital was ₹1 lakh—half from Panicker and four other investors who were all former HCL employees, and the other half, borrowed from a friend.

Panicker bought a used scooter to get around, but had to use it for only one year. That first year, the turnover was ₹51 lakh, with a profit of ₹7 lakh. The next year, he bought a company car. In the ninth year of business, aided by low-cost acquisitions, he achieved his goal of ₹100 crore revenue.

The success brought interest from private equity investors. ICICI Ventures in 1999 and Intel Capital in 2000 each invested $1.5 million. In 2000, the company finally ventured out of the domestic market into the software services outsourcing business, when lightning struck.

'We set up a software operation in Altanta,' Panicker says. 'We thought it would be easy. Then 9/11 happened. We had invested

4

$2-3 million setting up two-three offices. Everything collapsed. I decided to close down.'

With liabilities weighing on the company, and a public listing out of the question because of market conditions, Panicker turned to strategic partnerships.

In 2003, Frontline Technologies Corp. Ltd of Singapore got a 42 per cent stake in the company by acquiring ICICI Ventures' interest in Accel. In 2006, with the stock markets in better shape, and wanting to give an exit option to his employees, all of whom had stock options, Panicker listed the company on the stock exchanges.

British Telecommunications acquired Frontline in 2006 and bought some more equity from Accel to become the majority stakeholder in Accel Frontline.

'But then, BT had its own problems—there was the downturn in Europe, they wanted to reduce outsourcing in India,' Panicker says. 'In 2009–10, I realized they were not going to help grow the business.'

In August 2011, Accel acquired BT's stake in Accel Frontline. 'There's a difference between an entrepreneurial journey and a corporate journey,' Panicker says. 'A joint venture may not work out.'

Panicker is now in the process of amalgamating group companies including small acquisitions into two entities: an IT company and a media company, which will include units such as Accel Animation Studio.

'The challenge is that margins are very low in Indian IT,' Panicker says. 'Our challenge is how to make international margins available in the India market.'

The company's earnings before interest, tax, depreciation and amortization, or Ebitda, is only about 10-11 per cent of revenue, whereas many software companies make 20-22 per cent. To close the gap, Panicker plans to push for a bigger share of international business, concentrate on high-margin areas in India such as infrastructure management services, business process outsourcing and software services, while cutting down on the low-margin infrastructure management solutions business.

Panicker also wants to raise profits by cutting down on the cost of financing by paying off the company's current debt of about ₹100 crore. His goal is for Accel Frontline to be a zero-debt company in five years.

'We are starting Accel 2.0,' he says. 'In 1.0, we did a lot of experimentation. Now, we have things in place. It has taken the last 10 years to grow from ₹100 crore to ₹500 crore.' (The company had expected its revenue to grow to that figure by March 2012. With group companies being restructured this fiscal year, revenue in 2011–12 may be closer to ₹600 crore, according to Panicker.)

'Now I think we can grow it to ₹2,500 crore in the next five years.'

—❖—

Q&A
N. R. PANICKER

Have there been mistakes that have set you back?

Entrepreneurs are always ideas people. Many times, they don't get focused. At one point, we got into diversification and tried to do many things. In 1999–2000, we thought we should venture into software services. We set up a software operation in Atlanta in the US. Then 9/11 happened and everything crashed. We had just acquired Fujitsu ICIM (Ltd) of Pune in 2000. The US expansion was done through borrowed funds. When the market collapsed, that became a burden on the company. The company got into certain liabilities that had to be settled.

You have concentrated on the Indian software business. Do you think you may have missed the outsourcing boom?

I do feel that if I had to do this all over again, I probably would have done it differently. But you get entrenched in the India business and you cannot kill that and move on to something else. And we didn't have the required financial backing and needed a lot more back-office strength. This time, I think we are destined to succeed, because we have got all the ingredients to do that.

What has helped you make the transition from engineer to manager and leader?

That comes because of your ambition to achieve something. I have never gone to management school. I used to read balance sheets closely even when I was at HCL. I was part of the equity market cult in India in the 1970s. Finally, it's all about common sense. Of course, you need a lot of professionally qualified people in the system later when you want to build this into an institution.

What character traits have helped you in your entrepreneurial journey?

Perseverance. I never quit. Another thing is that I'm fundamentally a hard worker. Even at HCL, I was an intrapreneur—I was the hardest worker there. I did my work, and more than that.

After 20 years in the business, do you think you still have an appetite for risk?

I still have it. Some people say, 'At the age of 57, where is the energy left in you to drive this?' But there are people who start businesses at the age of 60 or 70 and make it big. That is not the criterion. What is important is—do you have vision, do you have passion and do you have a team with you?

2

Amara Raja Batteries Ltd

Creating opportunities
Ramachandra Galla

AMARA RAJA BATTERIES LTD

Founder: Ramachandra Gallla

Year of founding: 1985

Headquarters: Hyderabad

Website: www.amararaja.co.in

Area of business: Manufacturer of lead acid
storage batteries

Revenue: ₹2,076.5 crore in 2010–11

Profit: ₹148.1 crore after tax in 2010–11

Uniqueness

*Amara Raja Batteries has built a reputation as a quality
manufacturer and exporter of lead acid storage batteries.
The vertically integrated company sells a wide variety
of products catering to the needs of industrial,
automotive, office and residential markets.*

By Viswanath Pilla

First-generation entrepreneur Ramachandra Galla was already in his
mid-40s and ensconced in a lucrative professional career in the US
as an engineer at energy consultancy Sargent & Lundy, designing
nuclear and coal-fired power plants, when he was seized by the urge
to strike out on his own in the 1980s.

Galla, an active member of the Telugu Association of North America, a community based organization of non-resident Indians (NRIs),
was organizing a series of seminars at the time.

The topic of one seminar was identity issues Indian children had
to face growing up in the US and another was investment opportunities available back home for NRIs. The legwork involved interactions
with the Indian embassy in Washington and the industries department in New Delhi.

The seminars were duly held, but the research he did left a huge
impression on Galla. For the next few weeks, his conversations with

family and friends were all about entrepreneurship and moving back to India.

'When I first decided I should come back, my idea was to set up a manufacturing unit, given my engineering background,' says Galla, founder-chairman of Amara Raja Batteries Ltd.

Galla, who belongs to a middle-class agricultural family in Chittoor district of Andhra Pradesh, had a bachelor's degree in electrical engineering from Sri Venkateswara University in the town of Tirupati, and a master's in applied electronics from the University of Roorkee.

Galla went to the US in the mid-1960s for a master's degree in system sciences from Michigan State University. He started his professional career as an electrical engineer at United States Steel Corp., better known as US Steel, before moving on to Sargent & Lundy.

'I had left the country about 18 years ago; I didn't know what was happening in India. I took a six-week vacation, came to India to see the country, talk to various people and get an idea of what works here,' Galla recalls.

While Galla was still trying to crystallize a business idea, he got a chance to visit a thermal power station in Vijayawada city. The plant had just been built by the Andhra Pradesh government.

There, he found that the batteries used for backup systems in the power plant were based on primitive technology. Batteries are critical support systems in electric utilities for power backup.

'That was the time America had introduced a valve-regulated lead acid battery, the very latest technology, (which was) maintenance free,' Galla says. 'It was an evolutionary change in battery manufacturing. India hadn't heard about it.'

By the end of the visit to Vijayawada, Galla knew what he wanted to do: Set up an industrial battery manufacturing unit using the valve-regulated lead acid battery technology.

Galla went back to the US and struck a technical deal with US-based industrial power component maker GNB Inc. to manufacture batteries that entailed a lower maintenance cost, had a life expectancy that was 50 per cent more than conventional batteries and were eco-friendly.

He then faced twin setbacks. Galla's application seeking approval to set up his battery manufacturing unit was rejected by the department of industries and Industrial Development Bank of India turned down his loan request. The grounds were that there already was surplus manufacturing capacity and therefore no place for a new entrant.

He was also up against strong competition. Those days the Indian industrial battery market was dominated by Exide Batteries Ltd, Amco Batteries Ltd and Standard Batteries Ltd.

Galla says he did not lose hope. His confidence stemmed from the fact that the technology was far superior to that which went into conventional batteries.

'They rejected my applications because they did not understand the power of the underlying technology so I needed to convince them about the technology and its benefits vis-à-vis the competition,' he says.

Having ironed out the initial problems, Galla laid the foundation for Amara Raja Batteries in December 1985. He chose a small village called Karakambadi, an obscure location with no infrastructure to speak of, in Chittoor district to set up his factory.

'The decision to set up the factory in Chittoor district was a conscious one as I am emotionally connected to my native place; secondly, I wanted to create employment opportunities for people there,' Galla explains.

In the 1980s, the government used to be the major customer, if not the only one, for industrial batteries. To get government orders, the product needed to be tailored to official specifications. One of the conditions for approval was that a company should demonstrate that the product worked in India.

'It was just like chicken comes first or egg comes first,' smiles Galla.

Amara Raja took off and in 1992 Galla went public, using the proceeds for expansion. Throughout the 1990s, the company kept investing in capacity expansion and accessing technologies.

Sometime in the mid-1990s, the company realized that to sustain the business, it needed to diversify the product portfolio.

Automotive batteries seemed a logical area to move into but technology remained a key barrier for Amara Raja. Another challenge was that the automotive batteries business required significant investment in building the supply chain, dealership network and branding. Plus, the company had to customise batteries for a wide array of vehicles.

Amara Raja turned to battery maker Johnson Controls Inc. for a technology and business partner, given the US-based company's strong research and technology background. Johnson Controls wasn't too enthusiastic to begin with.

'They said India didn't even figure in their business strategy and the resources were already committed,' Galla recounts.

Eventually, they did reach an understanding. In December 1997, Johnson Controls purchased a 26 per cent stake in Amara Raja Batteries for around ₹75 lakh. The deal turned out to be Johnson's most successful overseas investment. Analysts say the 14-year-old partnership is also one of the most durable long-term relationships forged between an Indian and a foreign company.

In 1999, Amara Raja became the market leader in the industrial battery segment and set up its first automotive battery manufacturing unit built from scratch. By 2000, it had launched its first automotive battery under the brand name Amaron.

Galla credits his son Jayadev Galla for the company's entry into the automotive battery business and the venture with Johnson Controls.

For three years after the launch of the automotive battery business, the company bled on account of investments it made in building a supply chain, expanding its dealership footprint across the country and branding.

The investments paid off eventually. Revenue started surging in the 2000s as the telecommunications and automobile industries boomed in step with India's rapid economic growth.

Amara Raja Batteries clocked sales of ₹2,076.5 crore and net profit of ₹148 crore for the year ended 31 March 2011. The company generated 40 per cent of its revenue through exports.

Now 73, Galla likes to spend time with his family, read and take part in the corporate social responsibility (CSR) initiatives of his company. His son Jayadev takes care of day-to-day operations as managing director.

Q&A
RAMACHANDRA GALLLA

What are the challenges you faced while building your company?
We started our industry during the period of the licence raj. As you know, the biggest challenge those days was how to deal with the bureaucracy. It was completely paperwork and licence-oriented... But then you need to deal with it. I thought 'be a Roman in Rome.' First you have to learn how to adjust to the bureaucracy–smiling without getting frustrated.

Who is your role model?
I don't have any industry business role model. As an individual, my role model is my father-in-law. I have known him since high school and I hero-worshipped him. He always used to tell us we had to do something for society.

(Galla's father-in-law, the late Paturi Rajagopala Naidu, was a freedom fighter and an influential political figure in the Chittoor district of Andhra Pradesh's Rayalaseema region.)

What is the core objective and philosophy of Amara Raja?
Our intention is to bring about a transformation in the space we are presently in. That means transformation connected with technologies, transformation related to manufacturing, product transformation, market transformation.

The second thing is, create opportunity. There is no point in doing business if you don't provide opportunity for growth for all our people. Whatever you do, if you don't connect with society as a business model you can't sustain it.

What have been your key learnings?
I went to the US with $100. When I started business I started with meagre resources. I strongly believe that we need to first build strong fundamentals before we can build on top of it. I built my business brick by brick and step by step.

What is your advice to upcoming entrepreneurs?
They should be very objective. They should have a goal, and also they should define their philosophy. Construct the company step by step and systematically, so that the chances of failure will be less.

3

AppLabs Technologies Pvt. Ltd

A tech professional's entrepreneurial journey
Sashi Reddi

APPLABS TECHNOLOGIES PVT. LTD

Founder: Sashi Reddi

Year of founding: 2001

Headquarters: Philadelphia

Website: www.applabs.com

Area of business: IT testing services

Revenue: Not disclosed

Profit: Not disclosed

Uniqueness

Starting out as an IT testing services specialist, AppLabs was the world's largest independent software testing and quality management company till September 2011, when it was acquired by Computer Sciences Corp. It is the first independent testing services company to acquire CMMI (Capability Maturity Model Integration) Level 5 certification working with clients such as American Airlines, Experian, JPMorgan Chase, Royal Bank of Scotland and National Australia Bank, among others.

By Yogendra Kalavalapalli

Sashi Reddi started AppLabs Technologies Pvt. Ltd in 2001 when the markets were still trying to recover from the trauma of the dot-com boom that had gone bust the year before. He had been a victim of the dotcom bubble himself. His second venture, iCoop Inc., a group-buying portal on the lines of today's Groupon and Snapdeal, went belly-up, one of many Internet companies that collapsed during the period.

Wiser after the experience, Reddi wanted to venture into safer area in the third stop on his entrepreneurial journey. Information technology outsourcing seemed a logical business to get into, but Reddi realized that he would be up against entrenched giants. To try and beat them on their turf, he knew, would be virtual suicide. His offering had to be unique and in a niche business.

'I knew that I was quite late and probably being just another IT services player will not get any value and specialization,' says Reddi. 'So I thought long and hard about what is the specialization which, even if there are lot of other companies, there is always a need for people to do this.' He zeroed in on software testing services.

For the next 10 years, Reddi would dedicate himself to building his fortune around AppLabs until it was sold in September to Computer Sciences Corp. (CSC) for a price reported by VCCircle, the website that tracks venture capital and private equity (PE) deals, to be around ₹1,200 crore.

'I thought about testing for the reason that customers understand the benefit of separating development from testing. There will always be a need for people to do testing without any conflict of interest,' Reddi says. 'That worked out to be a good choice.'

From a three-member team working out of shared office space in Philadelphia, AppLabs grew to become a 2,500-employee-strong company spread across locations in India, the US and the UK specializing in software testing and quality management. It was rated the world's largest independent software testing company by analyst firm NelsonHall in 2010.

Operating in segments such as financial services, insurance, technology, retail, travel and healthcare and life sciences, AppLabs offered testing of software for functional utility, automation, performance, security, usability, and mobile and technology certification. Reddi's business model won the confidence of private equity firm WestBridge Capital, which invested around $20 million in AppLabs.

Along the way, AppLabs made strategic acquisitions to gain domain expertise and enter new markets. It a quired US-based software and hardware testing company KeyLabs Inc. in 2005, UK-based testing consultancy IS Integration Ltd in 2006 and Hyderabad-based developer of automated testing tools ValueMinds Solutions (P) Ltd in 2010.

Then came the company's sale to Falls Church, Virgina-based Computer Sciences Corp., giving private equity investors an exit opportunity. But AppLabs, Reddi says, was never meant to go that way. If not for the global recession of 2008, AppLabs would have been listed on the Nasdaq, the world's second largest stock exchange by market value.

'I think going public on the Nasdaq is a very big challenge and we wanted to take AppLabs public on the Nasdaq actually,' the 46-year-old says. 'That was the plan at that time.'

The downturn of 2008–2009 led to a slump in outsourcing projects for most IT companies, affecting the business as a whole, stalling the initial public offer (IPO) plan and preventing PE investors from gaining an exit opportunity.

Reddi's track record shows him to be a serial entrepreneur—he builds a business, scales it up and then sells it before going on to do something else. He sold his first venture EZPower Systems Inc., a developer of products for building and maintaining Web applications; after founding AppLabs, he set up computer game developer FXLabs Studios Pvt. Ltd and sold it.

This isn't a deliberate strategy, Reddi says.

'I think so far that is how it worked out, but who knows that may not be the case in the future,' he says. 'If you take AppLabs, for example, if not for the downturn we had in 2008, we were actually well on track to do an IPO because we were growing at a very nice rate, (we had) good customers and good investors.'

An entrepreneur's first company, he says, will either fail or be acquired. 'That's the typical outcome.'

FXLabs was a pet project of Reddi's. Two years after founding AppLabs, sensing an opportunity in the gaming market in India, he set up the company in 2003. He roped in experts from leading gaming companies such as Electronic Arts Inc. to set up a world-class gaming studio in Hyderabad.

'But unfortunately, the gaming market in India has not taken off. Even now, after so many years, it is still a very, very small business,' he says.

20

With not much traction in the business, coupled with rampant piracy in the market and low bandwidth speeds in the country, he sold FXLabs to video game maker Foundation 9 Entertainment Inc.

The fact that multinationals such as Computer Science Corp. and Foundation 9 Entertainment Inc. saw promise in Reddi's companies is testimony to the potential of his business ideas.

Reddi serves on the advisory boards of the Wharton Entrepreneurial Centre and Indian Institute of Technology (IIT), Hyderabad, and has also served on the board of advisors of his alma mater—Wharton School of Business. Flush with funds, he is currently investing in start-ups both in India and the US while helping AppLabs integrate with Computer Science Corp.

Reddi was born in Chennai in 1965 to a reasonably well-to-do family. His father worked with the Indian Tobacco Board and thanks to the nature of his job, the Reddis were constantly on the move. To ensure his academic career wasn't affected, Reddi was admitted to a boarding school—Lawrence School in Lovedale, Tamil Nadu.

He went on to graduate in computer science from IIT, Delhi. It was IIT that changed his attitude towards education after he realized the potential of technology and innovation. Soon after, he moved to the US to do his master's in computer science from New York University. He then enrolled for a PhD in the prestigious Wharton School, his doctoral thesis being on technology and strategy.

Reddi began his career as a consultant for Fortune 500 companies in the travel, financial services, automotive and consumer-packaged goods industries. He would have packed his bags for a consulting career in Hong Kong if not for a friend who insisted Reddi join him in a debut venture.

There has been no looking back since.

— ◆ —

Q&A
SASHI REDDI

What were the hurdles you faced initially?

Unfortunately for us, all three of us, it was the first company venture (EZPower Systems Inc.) that we were starting. We were all new to entrepreneurship. I was the CEO and my friend, who had the technology edge, was the CTO (chief technology officer). My other friend was the head of sales and marketing. That was the team.

So the biggest challenge there was how to raise money but we solved that by getting old friends and family to invest some amount. The other big challenge was understanding how do you go to market and win customers. My friend, who was the head of sales and marketing, had worked for some very large companies, but that experience does not fully translate when you are about a three-person, or in that case we were about a 20-person, company when you had to take your product to a customer. You don't have the big brand in India to somehow sell. But once we understood that we were quite successful, we signed up 30-odd customers including some five Fortune 500 companies.

We won a lot of awards for the technology. We were one of the first people to build a product on Java. This was in 1994–95. So we were very early. So all of this gave us good branding and visibility, lot of analysts talked very highly of us. Actually, we got two offers to buy out the company. We just picked one and sold out the company.

What are the lessons you have learnt in your entrepreneurial journey?

Even now, if I start something, yes, it's true it will be much easier but I know there will be new challenges, new things that could go wrong. There is no sure formula for success. And that is what, essentially, the make-up of an entrepreneur has to be—the understanding that things can and will go wrong. So one of the things is that we have to maintain a very optimistic view of life—that is the only thing that gets you through all the obstacles in life. There are a few key lessons I have learnt such as how to hire the right people, how to pick the right market, how to get the funding, all of these are good lessons but they do not assure success. There are still a lot of things that will go right or wrong.

Acquisitions played a key role in making AppLabs what it was. How important are acquisitions for any business?

In the case of AppLabs, the first acquisition worked out very well because we did it in the US. The second acquisition was much more of a challenge because I understand the US culture and I understand the Indian culture but when we were required to work with the UK that was new to me and that was a little bit of a challenge. It took us two years to get a good hand along with that acquisition. I think one of the things about acquisition is that the cultural factors are more important than just looking at the numbers and the effect on the market and things like that. Culture can make or break the acquisition. I think that as Indian companies buy foreign companies, cultural fit will make a huge difference in terms of what we will get out of the buy.

What do you mean by cultural factors?

It is in terms of countries—whether they have a flat or hierarchical structure, people speak up openly or not, the work ethic. For example, in the UK, after 5 p.m., no one is even going to answer their phone while in India and the US, you call somebody at 8 p.m. and they will be happy to take your call. But at the same time, for the time they work in the UK, they work very professionally. They will not waste a minute. There are slight differences... All these little things can lead to people feeling that they don't belong to this company or it can go the other way, where they feel comfortable and we get the full benefits of the acquisition. It is all based on how sensitive you are to different cultures and different working styles.

4

Bharat Biotech International Ltd

Krishna M. Ella

BHARAT BIOTECH INTERNATIONAL LTD

Founder: Krishna M. Ella

Year of founding: 1996

Headquarters: Hyderabad

Website: www.bharatbiotech.com

Area of business: Vaccines and bio-pharmaceuticals

Revenue: ₹270 crore in 2010–11

Profit: Not disclosed

Uniqueness

Bharat Biotech is among few companies that exclusively follow an innovation and discovery-led business model. The company is developing vaccines targeting diseases that include typhoid, malaria, Japanese encephalitis and chikungunya that are prevalent in the developing world. It supplies vaccines to governments and multilateral agencies with mass immunization programmes.

By Viswanath Pilla

Krishna M. Ella's earliest innovation came after a rejection. He had sought ₹12.5 crore from investors to fund a hepatitis-B vaccine programme. The venture capitalists thought his requirement ridiculously low.

'Merck had partnered with a Chinese company and they had put $100 million (₹500 crore) as investment using Merck technology... So that was the benchmark,' he recalls 15 years after he founded Bharat Biotech International Ltd with his wife Suchitra Ella.

To begin with, he needed about ₹6 crore to buy ultra-centrifuges, used to separate proteins from DNA. Without investor funding, he had to find an alternative. With expensive loans from banks and money scraped from savings, Ella devised what he calls the Himax technique.

The technique eliminated the use of toxic chemicals and increased the recovery of the hepatitis-B surface antigen by at least 85 per cent. It also helped Bharat Biotech bring down the cost of the vaccine as it could now do away with many of the costly methods used in the conventional processing. The company has filed a global patent for the process.

Ella continued hammering the point he had made to the investors, that he could work with small money. In October 1998, Bharat Biotech launched recombinant hepatitis-B vaccine Revac-B at $1 a dose. Larger companies were selling the vaccine at $23 a dose.

'Many thought my pricing is unsustainable, but even at that price we are making a decent margin,' Ella says with a grin. 'Focus on innovation from the outset is what led us to make affordable vaccines.'

Ella's making the affordable vaccine tag his own. Earlier this year, GlaxoSmithKline Plc. and Merck and Co. Inc. had to slash their prices on an infant diarrhoea vaccine after Bharat Biotech announced it would sell its version Rotavac, which it is developing, for $1 a dose in global markets. The vaccine sells for around $20 a dose in India.

Raised in an agricultural family in Tamil Nadu's Vellore district, Ella predictably earned a postgraduation degree in agriculture sciences. Then, on a Rotary Foundation scholarship, he moved to the US to acquire a doctorate in molecular biology from the University of Wisconsin. For a while, he taught as an assistant professor at the Medical University of South Carolina.

Then his mother called. She urged him to return to India.

On returning from the US, Ella took up a job as a scientist with Tata Tea Ltd, which he gave up to co-found Bharat Biotech in 1996. The company's initial focus was to build a vaccine to prevent the spread of the hepatitis-B virus, a cause of liver cancer.

Vaccine-making was a natural choice for Ella. His company has gone on to launch 14 vaccines and bio-pharmaceutical drugs, including vaccines to fight typhoid, polio and rabies.

In all these, Bharat Biotech has followed a high-volume, low-margin business model, focusing on exports to emerging markets, governments and multilateral agencies such as UNICEF, WHO, the Global Alliance for Vaccines and Immunization, and other bodies involved in mass immunization programmes.

The funds began flowing in. In 2005, ICICI Venture bought an 11% stake in Bharat Biotech for an undisclosed sum; the International Finance Corporation (IFC), an arm of the World Bank, bought a small stake for about $6 million.

But in the same year, the patent regime underwent a sea change. It was no longer possible to make inexpensive copycat vaccines using alternative manufacturing processes, a benefit enjoyed by Indian pharma and biotech companies for decades.

That was a defining moment for Bharat Biotech. The company had to go back to its roots, from being a maker of generic medicines to becoming an innovation-led firm. "If the company has to sustain for the next 50 years, then innovation and quality is the only way," Ella says.

The company has four vaccines in late-stage clinical trials that are done on humans. These include the Rotavac vaccine, which it is developing with a funding support of around ₹200 crore from the children's vaccine programme of the Bill and Melinda Gates Foundation. The other three vaccines are targeted at typhoid, Japanese encephalitis and infant diarrhoea. It also has a cardiovascular drug in late trials.

The Rotavac vaccine is expected to be launched by 2013.

Bharat Biotech is also developing vaccines to fight vector-borne diseases such as dengue, malaria, cholera, chikungunya and filaria. 'Our strategy is to develop vaccines for neglected diseases; people who suffer from these diseases are the poor who live in the emerging world. So it's not such a big concern for big pharma that largely focus on diseases more prevalent in the developed world,' says Ella.

Bharat Biotech plans to spend around $70 million in the next two years on research and development, or about one-third of the ₹270-crore revenue it made in 2010–11. It's that kind of focus that has fetched it 47 product patents worldwide.

Ella, on the side, is exploring his other facets. One of those is as a mentor to aspiring entrepreneurs. Ella is developing a plug-and-play incubation centre in Bhubaneswar that will include a research and development wing and an animal testing facility for biotech and pharma entrepreneurs in India's eastern regions. His other pursuits are in food processing and animal vaccines.

Q&A
KRISHNA M. ELLA

What challenges did you face as an entrepreneur?
As a technocrat entrepreneur, it's tough to face India as I need to understand the ecosystem of the country, the ecosystem of the financial system, innovation, human resources, and the regulatory system. And we were the second biotech company to be set up in India so it was much more challenging as the regulatory system was not fully evolved. We had to work with regulators and face the problem of finding the right solution for the country.

In addition, converting an idea into a product and deliverable thing was a huge challenge. In the biotechnology and vaccine field, the problem is not getting finance alone, but how to service the finance. If I take a loan, my product will only come after five-six years so the challenge is how to sustain the project for so long.

Can you illustrate an instance when you turned an adversity into an opportunity?
The first product was the hepatitis-B vaccine, which was launched by (former president) A.P.J. Abdul Kalam. The major challenge for us was we didn't have money, which was around ₹4-5 crore to buy ultra-centrifuges. Since we didn't have money to purchase ultra-centrifuges, we had to develop a new technology to make this vaccine. We developed Himax technology and got a global patent for it. That changed the whole dynamics of hepatitis-B vaccine productions globally. We produce the safest hepatitis-B vaccines in the world. We don't use any toxic chemicals. And we used less capital cost and also increased the yield by four-five times. These things helped us in increasing our profitability. Just making a product is not enough in this country, making the product in a cost-effective manner is the real challenge.

What do you think about innovation in the country?
It is unfortunate that neither a pharma company nor a biotech company in this country has launched a new molecule so far, which is not a good sign for a society like us. If you look back, India was the most innovative country

500-1,000 years ago. I think we have to get back to the culture of innovation. I think the new generation entrepreneurship will change that ecosystem in the country. I am a strong believer of intellectual property rights because IPR is going to help technocrat entrepreneurs like me. As a company we have already filed close to 50 patents in less than 10 years, out of which six-seven patents are in various stages of clinical trials.

What is your strategy for Bharat Biotech?

My model is very simple. How this company Bharat Biotech can sustain the business for the next 50 years. One nice thing about vaccine, it doesn't get replaced that easily unlike the pharmaceutical industry, where a new drug replaces the old drug. How do you build that imagination in this company, where you can sustain for the next 50 years?

The second strategy is how do you bring new vaccines which are more important for the developing world, and particularly so for India. We are identifying the diseases, working on innovative approaches and building intellectual property.

What is the most satisfying moment of your entrepreneurial journey?

Today, hepatitis-B vaccine is sold (at) less than (what) a water bottle costs. So somebody (who) can offer to buy a water bottle can offer to give hepatitis-B vaccine, and same is the case with the typhoid vaccine. When we launched hepatitis-B vaccine, GSK was selling it at $35-40 a dose. Today, we are selling it for less than a dollar a dose. That's the most satisfying moment for me.

What is your advice to upcoming entrepreneurs?

Don't copy from Bharat Biotech. Suppose I had done rabies vaccine and somebody wants to do rabies vaccine too, it'd be foolish. My capacity is huge, I have written off depreciation and (am) very competitive; there is no point in copying the same vaccine. Instead of that, they should take some other problem of society and work on it.

And they don't have to set up a manufacturing plant. Suppose you are good at molecular biology, you can develop a vaccine candidate and license it for development and work with a manufacturing company for production. Start concentrating on another candidate. Work in partnerships. There is no point in duplicating the entire value chain.

5

Consim Info Pvt. Ltd

The matchmaker
Murugavel Janakiraman

CONSIM INFO PVT. LTD

(Promoters of BharatMatrimony.com)

Founder: Murugavel Janakiraman

Year of founding: 2000

Headquarters: Chennai

Website: www.consim.com

Area of business: Online classifieds,
primarily matchmaking services

Revenue: Not disclosed

Profit: Not disclosed

Uniqueness

*The company has the early mover advantage in online
matrimonial classifieds, but what sets it apart is cultural
sensitivity, illustrated by features such as optional password
protection for women's photographs.*

By Vidya Padmanabhan

In the middle of 2001, Murugavel Janakiraman came to a critical juncture in his life. The dotcom bust had just seen him getting laid off from his job as a software consultant in the US. He was newly married, had a house under construction in India and there were loans to pay. Under the circumstances, he was lucky to get a job offer from an old employer.

He turned it down. Instead, he took a leap of faith and started working full-time on what had until then been a part-time business.

The gamble paid off. Over the following decade, Janakiraman's little business became key in helping one of the most traditional activities underpinning Indian society—the search for a suitable boy or girl—migrate online. Today, his company, Consim Info Pvt. Ltd, owns a cluster of matchmaking websites, apart from his flagship creation BharatMatrimony.com. The company, which also runs job and property portals, has grown from one to more than 2,200 people, and has been endorsed by private equity investors with about $20 million in funding.

But the growth has not been without its rough periods, such as during the 2008 global economic slump, when Janakiraman was forced to lay off nearly 300 people. However, he views even the rocky stretches as stepping stones.

'I had to manage internal conditions and keep people motivated, I had to manage market conditions, board expectations,' says Janakiraman, a boyish-looking 40-year-old. 'But it was a superb experience. Thank God for that experience—that's when this entrepreneur became a CEO.'

Janakiraman is quick to see the positive outcomes of adversity. For instance, though the limited education of his father, a manual labourer, and his mother, a housewife, may have placed him at a disadvantage growing up, it also liberated him to make his own career decisions, he says.

He grew up in a 300 sq.ft. home in a working class neighbourhood of Chennai near the city's harbour, where his father worked. The only member of his immediate family to go to high school—his first, daunting experience with English-medium instruction—and the second person among his relatives to go to college, he stumbled into a bachelor's programme in statistics at Chennai's Presidency College. He followed this with a master's in computer applications, and later worked as a computer consultant in Singapore and in the US.

It was in America, in 1996, staying up until 4 a.m. after his regular workday and working during weekends, that he started developing a Tamil website with applications such as a daily Tamil calendar and greeting cards. His entrepreneurial inclination, which had previously been restricted to freewheeling discussions with friends in college, was growing stronger, and he promoted his site through fliers in grocery stores in New Jersey, where he lived at that time, and through emails to friends.

In 1999, he found that the matrimonial section of his site was growing in popularity, and that was a lightbulb moment for Janakiraman. The next year he launched separate matrimonial websites for the Tamil and Telugu communities, apart from the umbrella website BharatMatrimony.com.

He decided right away to charge fees for his matchmaking service, which involved hosting profiles of prospective brides and grooms grouped by mother tongue, despite criticism against the move. 'Initially there were complaints from people,' he says. 'They said, "Everything on the Internet is free. How can you charge?" But I was firm that if you want to create a good service, you have to charge for it.'

Janakiraman's instinct served him well. The service found takers, even with the fee. Having started with ₹300 for one year for the standard service, BharatMatrimony now charges ₹2,700 for three months.

Returning to India in 2004 to manage the growing business, Janakiraman ran into the problem of Indian credit card usage. Or rather the lack of it. To get around this, he had to go offline and set up brick-and-mortar payment collection centres around the country. There are 120 retail centres around the country now, and the company expects to have 200 by March 2012.

Situated in the prime real estate of online classifieds just as private equity investor interest in India was surging, BharatMatrimony attracted an investment of $8.65 million from Yahoo Inc. and Canaan Partners in 2006. The money was badly needed.

'If I had not raised the money, I would have been finished. There was competition,' Janakiraman says. 'So we raised the money—we made a lot of mistakes, also grew, and here we are.'

The company received a second round of funding worth $11.65 million from the Mayfield Fund and Canaan in 2008. Then came the global economic crisis, and with it, a directive from the company's board that BharatMatrimony had to cut its monthly expenses by ₹1.5 crore to ₹5 crore within five months.

'I was leveraging on technical strengths, product strengths,' Janakiraman says. 'The rest was managed by other people. So there were a lot of gaps in the system—in finance, efficiency, and so on. A lot of flab got added because we wanted to grow.'

He had to go through his expenses with a fine-toothed comb to cut the flab. That was when the lay-offs occurred. 'It was a lot of pressure,' he says. 'I would get up at 4 in the morning and wonder what was going to happen.'

But the pressure moulded him into the CEO his title proclaimed him to be, he says. The company met its cost-cutting target, and he understood how to run a business efficiently.

In the decade since BharatMatrimony was launched, several rivals have come to occupy the market that the Janakiraman helped create. How does he stay in the front of the pack?

'It's continuous innovation,' he says. Three years ago, BharatMatrimony was the only entity in the company. Today, it has a matchmaking service with personal assistance dubbed PrivilegeMatrimony. com, which charges ₹19,000 per year, and a website for high-networth individuals, EliteMatrimony.com, where the fee is ₹50,000 for three months. In 2011, it ventured overseas, launching services in Pakistan, Bangladesh and Sri Lanka.

Janakiraman has also been savvy about plugging gaps in the market—he recently launched CommunityMatrimony.com, a cluster of websites with profiles grouped by community (Nair, Kayastha, etc.) rather than language.

BharatMatrimony currently enjoys more than two million active users—those who have logged on during the last six months—according to Janakiraman, while 1 million actively use CommunityMatrimony.com.

Revenue grew 50 per cent in 2010–11 and is on track for a similar rate of expansion in 2011–12, he says, while declining to elaborate on the amount of the money the company makes.

'We are absolutely on our way to creating something big,' he says. 'We are on the move.'

Q&A
MURUGAVEL JANAKIRAMAN

What character traits helped in your entrepreneurial journey?
I have leveraged my strengths—enthusiasm and energy, honesty, and the ability to get along with people. I always understood the power of networking. I got my first job because of the network I developed. So I've always been a person who has a good network of friends and I maintain those relationships.

Have there been missteps along the way?
You have ₹40 crore sitting in the bank (after the first round of private equity funding in 2006). You want to grow. You put the money in things without thinking about return on investment, just wanting to grow the business. Within one year, the ₹40 crore is gone. Thankfully, the business grew at a much better pace because of the investments we made. We got a second round of funding (in 2008) with a good valuation.

Any experience that helped you become a better businessperson?
It was the recession that really changed me from entrepreneur to CEO. In 2008, when the slowdown happened, the board came in and said if we continued to spend the way we were doing, we couldn't survive for a very long time. This has always been a cash-in-advance business. So cash flow is never a problem. The question is how to efficiently manage this cash flow. I went through each and every cost—telephone costs, manpower costs. It was a challenging period—we had to let go of people. But it was a beautiful experience. I understood how to run a business efficiently.

Who are your role models?
Steve Jobs (of Apple Inc.)—I wish I had met him in person; N.R. Narayana Murthy (of Infosys Ltd), Dr. A.P.J. Abdul Kalam (former president). But I look for inspiration everywhere. I look for ideas even in my daughter's pre-KG reports that her school sends home.

Have you looked outside your core category, matrimony, for growth?

At one point, in 2007–08, we thought jobs was a bigger category, and it is. But for me, the bigger revelation has been that growth is limited only by our ability to innovate. In this category (matrimony), we can grow at a much faster pace.

6

CGH Earth Group of Hotels

When less is more
Jose Dominic

CGH EARTH GROUP OF HOTELS
(formerly Casino Group of Hotels)

Founder: Dominic Joseph Sr

Year of founding: 1954

Headquarters: Kochi

Website: www.cghearth.com

Area of business: Ethnic hotels and resorts

Revenue: ₹75 crore

Profit: Not disclosed

Uniqueness
*Taking to heart the concept of less is more was unheard
of in the hotel industry back in the late 1980s. Having
successfully marketed luxury without televisions and room
service, CGH Earth dares to put the customer last.*

By Amritha Venketakrishnan

Choosing between running luxury hotels in Kerala, the self-proclaimed God's own country, and being a chartered accountant in Mumbai can't really be a difficult call to make.

In 1974, Jose Dominic, now chief executive officer of the ₹75 crore CGH Earth, faced such a choice. Under family pressure, he reluctantly opted to go to Kerala.

'I wrote out a resignation letter and kept it in my pocket for well over a month before I handed it in (to the chartered accountancy firm),' says the 60-year-old Dominic.

Having made the decision, it's not one he regrets now.

The family-run CGH Earth was started by Dominic's father in 1954, when he opened the doors of Casino restaurant on Willingdon Island, Kochi, to hungry sailors. The company has expanded to manage a dozen properties, including the much-coveted Bangaram Island in Lakshadweep that the family bid for successfully in

1988; it is currently shut following the non-renewal of a lease that is being contested in court.

The group's experience in running and maintaining the island resort was key to shaping the philosophy of its hospitality business, with ecological and community sensitivity forming the core.

'We kept tabs on the amount of water we consumed, sound levels, ecological preservation...measures that were far ahead of their time,' Dominic says. 'So, in short, what happened is that ecology and the local community were given priority over the customer. That was a completely different paradigm.'

Still, the customers came and were willing to pay five-star rates for the resort in admiration of its location and beauty. The lessons from Bangaram were parlayed into another resort that came up soon after, called Spice Village at Thekkady in Kerala. While Bangaram didn't have amenities such as television because of the logistical problems associated with providing such services in remote locations, Spice Village adopted it as an additional selling point after much debate.

'The most difficult decision was to keep the television out,' says Dominic. 'Most hotels would say that the television must be offered, but we took TV out.'

Dominic has a simple plan to manage costs and pricing. He employs local labour, uses easily available building material and depends on the area's design aesthetics to build a property. This keeps costs low, improves the appeal of the rooms that are seen as an ethnic experience and allows CGH to charge a higher room rate.

'The architects of the property were the Mannan tribe who are the indigenous people of Thekkady, Periyar and the offering was nature,' Dominic says. 'We offered an engaging experience in a way that was non-consumptive and non-intrusive to the surrounding forest. All this was changing the way business was done. It continued to attract people who came to enjoy this.'

So where competitors were building property in the area at seven times the price, CGH kept its costs low and managed to make profits.

The family was always on the lookout for new opportunities. In the early 1990s, the Dominic brothers saw old Kerala homes being broken to make the way for ugly modern structures, with the money coming from Malayalees working in West Asia. Dominic picked up one such traditional Kerala home and created Coconut Lagoon, the first resort on the backwaters.

The staff were people from the local community dressed in their traditional attire and the food was Kerala cuisine, instead of the European, Chinese, Indian and continental fare offered everywhere else.

'Ordinary people, ordinary food, ordinary architecture,' Dominic says. 'It seemed to attract the top-spending travellers, much like (at) Bangaram Island and Spice Village. And so the ordinary became extraordinary. Coconut Lagoon set the backwaters on fire.'

More importantly, Dominic reminisces that the fear of competing with international five-star chains and their standard, staple and boring offerings, was conquered.

'This was the beginning of Kerala tourism growth...of local entrepreneurs doing what they could, which was small-scale, local and at a level they could afford,' Dominic says. 'Indigenous and small could still be world-class. So I think this was the biggest contribution of the CGH group.'

In 2003, Dominic changed the name of the Casino Group of Hotels to CGH Earth, thus ridding it of the name's associations with gambling and emphasizing the company's environmental consciousness. He continued expanding the brand to focus on health and well-being through the establishment of Kalari Kovilakom, which offered Ayurveda retreats complete with diet therapies and massages, with a minimum stay of two weeks.

Dominic recalls a quote by the late Apple Inc. CEO Steve Jobs to explain his point.

'Like Jobs says, "You cannot just ask customers what they want and then try to give that to them",' says Dominic, explaining that companies have to think beyond the customer's imagination.

He explained his philosophy with a story.

There was a Gujarati family that stayed at three CGH Earth properties on a vacation. The husband complained incessantly to the staff about the absence of a TV and looked down on the group's concept of luxury without the idiot box.

'But at the end of his trip he wrote a very nice letter, where he said that for the first time for a whole week he had not watched television and it was the first time he spoke at length to his son,' Dominic says. The letter ended with a plea to never put a TV in any of his resorts.

CGH Earth is now looking to expand in North India and has set its sights set on the Andaman and Nicobar islands.

The five brothers who run the group have their differences, but in the end always iron them out.

'The family at large is the biggest asset and also the biggest liability,' Dominic says. 'It slows down, it needs consent and it needs consensus. You need to adapt and accept differences. You can't carry on regardless. It means everybody should be carried with you. This is our strength too.'

The challenge now is to find spaces for the next generation to spread their wings, he says.

Q&A
JOSE DOMINIC

When you took up your father's business, what went through your mind?

I recall one event where I met one of my clients at the (accounting) firm who was a senior leader in hospitality, and told him that I would be joining my father. But he cautioned me against giving up my career in finance to run a hotel. He says for a hotel to be successful you need two things: First, you must be part of a large chain, and second, you need to have size, at least 100-200 rooms.

My father's hotel had neither. That disappointed and discouraged me. Anyway, I came back and joined the business and promised myself two years, but got sucked into the system and stayed on. I do not regret it.

In 1988, the government decided to privatize the Bangaram Island. How was your offering different?

When the bid was announced, the grapevine said that all the big boys, Taj, Leela etc., were interested. So I knew my chances were small.

My proposal, simply stated, was: don't spoil this island with another hotel. Clean up and tidy up whatever there is (of the government hotel there) and make it more appropriate for the offering. There are two reasons for doing that. First, I do not have the crores to do anything else. Second, logically, I couldn't imagine why somebody would come all the way from London or Frankfurt to stay at another hotel. Here was a spectacular island and the pull of it was so dramatic. So a unique stay on the island was (what was needed).

What were the challenges you faced after setting up in Bangaram Island?

Our tour operators would say, 'What is this, there are no facilities and you are charging so much ($180 a night)?' But the customer was willing to pay and visit the island. This experience gave us the encouragement and the knowledge that there is another way. We brought this back to the mainland.

How have holidays changed?

We believe we are in a post-modern phase of holidays, where the offer is experience and with the customer you would dare say he is not necessarily the king.

The king is the environment and the local community and the customer is happiest knowing that these are rated above him. We are, therefore, putting heavy stress on what we call responsible tourism or eco-tourism. We want to lift the bar of the holiday and provide a transformational experience, which the customer can take back, not just memories or sightseeing. For example, the television is out. Instead we have butterfly parks.

Going forward, what can we expect from CGH Earth?

Our canvas is India and nations surrounding the subcontinent, be it Oman, Dubai, Mauritius, Maldives or Sri Lanka.

So far we have been owning or leasing our properties and now we are moving into managing properties. Now we will have to work with partners.

We will try to push the scale of our operations through private equity first and then maybe look at going public.

7

DQ Entertainment International Ltd

'I am living my dream'
Tapaas Chakravarti

DQ ENTERTAINMENT INTERNATIONAL LTD

Founder: Tapaas Chakravarti

Year of founding: 2001

Headquarters: Hyderabad

Website: www.dqentertainment.com

Area of business: Animation

Revenue: ₹161.70 crore in 2010–11

Profit: ₹13.29 crore in 2010–11

Uniqueness

DQ Entertainment's USP comes from the ability to develop global networking with marquee broadcasters, distributors, aggregators, producers and funding agencies supported by putting together the best of creative talents from the US, France, the UK, India and the Philippines. Its production pipeline is completely covered for the next three years of pure service or co-production service orders. It also licenses and merchandises its intellectual property.

By Yogendra Kalavalapalli

When little Tapaas met Mowgli and his friends the first time he read Rudyard Kipling's *The Jungle Book* as a child, he had no idea the "man-cub" would one day swing his fortunes.

Almost 40 years later, sitting in his plush corporate office in Hyderabad, a proud Emmy standing tall among the awards behind his desk, Tapaas Chakravarti, chief executive officer and chairman, DQ Entertainment International Ltd, is an animated eight-year-old when he talks about Mowgli and his companions in the forest, who, among many other characters, have catapulted DQ Entertainment to the top league animation companies in the world.

No surprise then when he picks out Mowgli as his favourite creation. 'Jungle Book was there with me in my heart when I was hardly seven years old,' he says. *The Jungle Book*, one of the company's most

47

cherished intellectual properties, will be featured on television in 160 countries. DQ Entertainment also owns intellectual property for popular characters such as Peter Pan, Ironman (in collaboration with Marvel Comics), Casper the friendly ghost, Charlie Chaplin, Lassie and Indian characters like Balkand, Ravan and Omkar—all supported by national and international broadcasters, distributors and licensees.

DQ Entertainment's claim to fame came the day it won India its first Emmy, considered the Oscars of television, for *Tutenstein*, a series it co-produced with US-based Porchlight Entertainments for Discovery Kids, USA. It also has the honour of being nominated 11 times for the awards.

From a middle-class boy who caught up with his daily dose of comics secretly under the hood of a bedsheet to a globe-trotting CEO who stays awake till 1 a.m. talking to clients and partners in the West, Chakravarti has come a long way.

His father worked with Indian Railways and the Chakravartis were constantly on the move, travelling throughout Uttar Pardesh—Gorakhpur, Bareilley, Lucknow and Varanasi. Like most middle-class families in India, his parents, too, harboured dreams of seeing their son in the echelons of power, as an Indian Administrative Service officer. But Chakravarti had other aspirations.

'I knew very well what kind of business it will be. I knew that it was something to do with arts, something to do with cartoons, but whether it is animation or something else, I had no idea then,' he says of his childhood ambitions. It was a case study during his master of business administration (MBA) course at Benares Hindu University that firmed up Chakravarti's entrepreneurial resolve. 'I did not want to be a small trader or small entrepreneur,' he says. 'My dreams were very big.'

But Chakravarti was practical. Growing up in a government official's household meant he had no inkling of the workings of a businessperson; neither was there adequate capital to back him up. Education and experience, Chakravarti knew, held the key to his dreams. 'I understood very clearly that if I do not have quality education, and by education I also mean working in four-five high quality organizations, I will never learn how organizations are built,' he says. 'So I decided that everything else has to be on the back burner.'

And so, for a brief period at the start of his career, he worked with four companies including Coats (India), Sandoz India Ltd and STPI India, picking them out carefully: they had to give him opportunities to work in different functions and the positions should be based in India. As he moved up the ladder, he learnt first-hand how companies are built, manpower managed, how human resources function, how organizational dynamics work, how an organization's dynamics work with a client's, and the importance of financial discipline.

In the early 1990s, around the time India was opening up its economy, Chakravarti knew the time had come. He co-founded Data Quest Management and Communications with two partners in 1991, offering advisory services in helping entrepreneurs set up companies and raise funds, among other consultancy services. In the process, he learnt the ropes of building a company, raising investment from various sources, scaling a business and so on. His first venture was a success but during the mid-1990s Chakravarti knew he had to move on. There was a childhood dream to be realized.

During the course of his consulting career Chakravarti met different people but none impressed him as much as Rusi Brij, a senior Satyam Computer Services Ltd executive who joined information technology services provider Hexaware Technologies Ltd In Brij, Chakravarti found not just a potential business partner but also a friend whom he admired and respected. Brij, vice-chairman and chief executive officer of Hexaware Technologies, died in 2009 after battling cancer.

DQ Entertainment, a financial and management consultancy to begin with, commenced animation production in 2001, establishing a 2D animation studio in 2002. When he ventured into the animation outsourcing business, Chakravarti realized he had a serious problem to grapple with: even though the projects were coming in, quality animators were hard to come by. This he overcame by instituting an in-house animation training centre. The six centres of DQ School of Visual Arts, managed by his wife Rashmi Chakravarti, have produced 4,000 animators so far, many of whom were absorbed by the parent company. The training division, which Chakravarti describes as a 'core strength' of DQ Entertainment, acts as a constant feeder ensuring work is never disrupted in this human resource intensive industry. 'This became a hallmark for our capability to scale.' With 3,200 employees in India and 300 freelancers specializing in hand-drawn 2D animation in Manila, DQ Entertainment claims to be the world's largest linear animation company in terms of human capacity.

Meanwhile, the initial investment of ₹1 crore pooled from Chakravarti's and Brij's savings was fast running out and the company needed to infuse capital to scale up the business, which was when private equity firms stepped in. Between 2003 and 2005, DQ Entertainment raised $8 million from five investors—IL&FS Investment Managers, India Value Funds USA, International Finance Corporation Washington, iLabs Venture Capital Fund and TDA Capital Partners. The funds brought stability to the business as its revenue grew at a 35 per cent compound annual growth rate (CAGR) year-on-year.

In December 2007, soon after the crash of Lehman Brothers Holdings Inc.—a bad time to go public—the company listed on the Alternative Investment Market (AIM) of the London Stock Exchange primarily to provide an exit route for its investors. 'I believe that they got approximately five times their investment and exited happily, while three of them did not exit fully and remain part of the London Stock Exchange public portfolio,' he says.

Attempts to go public in India in 2008–09 remained unfruitful owing to the tough market conditions, but by 2010 the company had to raise funds to grow. When DQ Entertainment went public in March 2010 on BSE, it was oversubscribed 87 times. The money went into setting up 55,000 sq. ft of office space housing 1,800 employees. 'This listing gave that muscle and power to the company for creating, producing and marketing great intellectual property worldwide,' says Chakravarti, now a minority shareholder in the company. That's the origin of the Jungle Book television series, he says.

Intellectual property, Chakravarti knew, was the key to survival in an industry where low price levels prevailed in a market of too many service companies. 'The day I founded this company I knew we had to bring big brands, produce it as our own properties, our own designs, our own stories, patent them and market them,' he says. 'Asian animation industry can never become big or an individual company cannot become large until and unless they own intellectual properties and exploit them the way the Disneys of the world, Cartoon Networks of the world, or Dreamworks of the world have done.'

With focus on long-term growth, the entertainment company went about building 'big brand IPs'. Today, it has 35 well-known intellectual properties—the likes of Peter Pan, Jungle Book (second season), Charlie Chaplin, Casper, Lassie and Iron Man—in various stages of development covering the next five years of production. Having built intellectual property, DQ Entertainment is in the process of monetising its brands by licensing them and developing merchandise, which it believes will ensure sustained, long-term upstream revenues.

Merchandising and licensing, currently contributing 20 per cent of the company's revenues, are growing very rapidly and in the next five years, declares Chakravarti, will surpass the other revenue streams of the company. 'That's the power of IP. You own the intellectual property and then you can do so much merchandising for that.' For now, about 60 per cent of the revenue comes from intellectual property service while the rest is contributed by outsourced projects. Walt Disney Television Animation, Nickelodeon Animation Studios Inc., Electronic Arts Inc., Marvel Animation Inc., American Greetings Corp., NBC-Universal and the British Broadcasting Corp. are among DQ Entertainment's major clients.

Intellectual property aside, DQ Entertainment has its order book full with characters such as Little Prince, Robin Hood and Little Nick covering the next three years of shopfloor capacity. At the same time, it is taking a 'big leap' to produce 3D stereoscopic feature films of Jungle Book (slated for a 2014 release), Peter Pan (2015), and Phoenix and the Flying Carpet (2015), with a working budget of $40 million each. Not willing to take a chance, he is roping in top technicians for the projects, the likes of Billy Frolick (a co-writer of animated movie Madagascar). Eric Rollman, president of Marvel Animation Inc., will be executive producer for Jungle Book and Peter Pan, in various stages of development. 'Development is being funded by internal cash flow and the entire production will be funded by our banks based on the strategic and distribution deals we are finalizing worldwide,' Chakravarti says.

His dream? 'We want to be among the top 10 studios in the world, which is a huge leap and this can only happen with television, feature films and gaming worldwide along with licensing, merchandising and publishing,' he says.

Q&A
TAPAAS CHAKRAVARTI

What is DQ's style of animation?

Sometimes it is fuller, smooth animation, sometimes snappy—it is acting-based animation. All our intellectual properties are character-based storytelling, right amount of humour and non-stop action with deep inter-character relationships. This defines our style of animation, which is very similar to the animation created by the top studios in the world. To do so we hire writers, designers, directors, art directors, voice artists and musicians from Paris, London and Los Angeles so that our IP offering is homogeneous with what is happening there.

Which are your favourite characters among those you have created?

I think one of the most interesting characters is Mowgli. How the child survived in a jungle against a formidable enemy like Sher Khan. His friendship, his way of life and the way he can help a friend, he does not hesitate helping even an enemy in need, that's the character. He has got a very strong character. Another lovable character for me is Peter Pan, the boy who never grew up. Everybody's fantasy is we should never grow and we should remain at whatever age we are. There is so much to learn or unlearn from him.

What were the difficulties you overcame?

The day I founded this company I knew we had to bring big brands, produce it as our own properties, our own designs, our own stories, patent them and market them. But before we reached that stage—and that's a critical stage to reach—we had to develop manpower, train manpower, retain manpower and reach the quality which will be comparable with the best in the world, these were the challenges. It took us four-five years' time to reach that stage. Once we reached that stage, we started moving faster.

Where do you think the animation industry is headed?

Animation industry, if you go by the statistics, is a little over $60 billion industry. This includes television, movies, box office, licensing, merchandising, publications and gaming. And 45 per cent component of that is feature films alone. We don't have 10 or 12 animation feature films a year but they are bringing in multi-billion-dollar revenues together. Feature film side of the animation industry is growing very rapidly. But it can be handled only by very large, high quality companies. The television side is growing slowly for the last two-three years. With our multiple partnerships worldwide for television we have been able to keep up our growth but worldwide television growth has come down compared with what it was four-five years back. But during the last Cannes festival we have seen there is again a rise in the television business also. Online content, IPTV and digital content distribution is further increasing the requirement of animation worldwide. Animation for applications on iPad and Android devices is also on the rise. But there will be fewer but stronger players in the market as it always happens after recession and they will lead the industry to much greater glory.

What are the challenges facing the Indian animation industry?

Unfortunately, the Indian animation industry has never received the backing of the cultural, information & broadcasting or the finance ministry the way our counterparts in France, Canada, South Korea, Singapore, Malaysia and Japan have received. The industry did not even get its own status and is considered as (part of the) IT industry... If some good policies come in, like removal of service tax, removal of excise and import duties, reduced corporate tax for this new and growing industry, and then the regime of providing equity funding for creating intellectual properties for India as well as for global market, will all help this industry to grow into a global giant. The potential has been exploited by the entrepreneurs themselves on their strength without any governmental support. You can imagine that if the government comes forward and gives us support, the way it supported the IT industry and other industries, this industry can also become a multi-billion dollar industry in India.

8

Eka Software Solutions Pvt. Ltd

'The ability to persevere is the key to success'
Manav Garg

EKA SOFTWARE SOLUTIONS PVT. LTD

Founder: Manav Garg

Year of founding: 2004

Headquarters: Bangalore

Website: www.ekaplus.com

Area of business: Commodity trading and
risk management software

Revenue: $9 million in 2010–11;
$14 million projected for 2011–12

Profit: Not disclosed

Uniqueness

*Eka's software is the only web-based product in the
commodity trading and risk management space in India.
The company, among a few software product firms in
the country, aims to provide end-to-end supply chain
management and is eyeing annual revenue of about
$100 million in 3-4 years.*

By Sridhar K. Chari

Stock, bond, and commodity traders can be quite cerebral, with a finely tuned appreciation of risk. That understanding of risk taking stood Manav Garg in good stead as he made the transition from a successful coffee trader to an entrepreneur selling commodity and risk management software to billion dollar companies worldwide.

'We are changing the product landscape in India,' says 37-year-old Garg, matter-of-factly and without smacking of hubris. The passion for risk-taking, entrepreneurship, and making software products is evident, as is an acute sense of just how far India still has to travel in this area.

Garg is chief executive of Eka Software Solutions Pvt. Ltd, which he founded in 2004. The firm has 230 employees and 25 clients, many of these making above $10 billion in annual revenue.

Eka itself made $9 million in revenue in fiscal 2011, with operating margins at a healthy 30 per cent.

Garg is eyeing a 50 per cent jump, hoping to close fiscal 2012 with $14 million in revenue. And he is confident that in three to four years, Eka will cross the $100 million mark.

'We have got so far in this market because we are looking at solutions for the entire supply chain. That is how you get optimization and risk management in this business,' he says. 'Our solution is new, so the technology is fresh, the architecture is clean, and we are the only web-based product solution (company), unlike the client-server based technologies that exist.'

Eka is active in three segments—agricultural commodities, metals and mining, and energy.

For many of its clients, it helps replace in-house legacy software. After all, notes Garg, the era of trading on paper and Excel sheets wasn't so long ago.

The firm, aiming to 'go deeper' in the supply chain, as Garg puts it, is scouting for acquisitions in resource-rich geographies such as Brazil and Australia. It already has offices in Connecticut in the US, London, Adelaide and Venezuela.

Eka will have to add muscle fast to catch up with competition from vendors like Triple Point Technology Inc. and SunGard, both larger, global companies based in the US.

Garg grew up in Punjab, where his father worked at a factory of food company Nestle SA. He graduated as an engineer from the National Institute of Technology, Jalandhar, and did an MBA at the Indian Institute of Foreign Trade (IIFT) in New Delhi.

Soon after, in 1998, he started as a commodity trader in Singapore with the G. Premjee group. After two years, however, the risk taker in him and the 'urge to create something' came to the fore.

He quit his high-paying job, startling family and friends, and using the money he had saved, hit the road, meeting companies and validating the idea in his mind.

'Many of my IIFT classmates were abroad, doing very well, and they said "why don't you come over". But I wanted to do something else with my life.'

As a coffee trader, he had first-hand knowledge of the intricacies of commodity trading, its volatility, the uncertainty, the spectrum of risks spanning seasons, time zones, and geographies; not to mention politics and policies that needed to be monitored and responded to in real time.

Surely, he thought, there must be better ways than using spreadsheets to make decisions. How about creating a web-based solution that would optimize results for companies?

Two years later, he convinced the chairman of the group he quit to give him $5 million, and Eka was born. Later came an infusion of $10 million from Nexus Venture Partners.

His primary revenue model is software licensing—a per-user, perpetual licence. A few months ago, Eka launched an initiative for a Software-as-a-Service (SaaS) model for medium-sized companies.

In this model, the software, hosted on distant servers, is delivered over the web on a pay-as-you-use basis. SaaS is an emergent model, attractive to smaller companies that cannot budget for large, licensing expenditure and would like to pay on actual usage.

Garg believes it is his 'dogged determination' that saw him through the early years. Today, he is also an angel investor. 'I would rather fund an entrepreneur than buy a BMW,' he says. 'Look at the success of IT services companies and professionals. Some of that money needs to come back into the system. And there is no deficit of ideas. They need to be shaped.'

While it is often emphasized that entrepreneurship is about risk taking and shedding the fear of failure, the culture of risk taking has to take hold across the ecosystem, he says. 'Even venture capitalists here are risk averse. That has to change.'

The Silicon Valley is successful as a haven for entrepreneurs because risk and failure are tolerated. 'We have a Facebook today but there are hundreds of companies which started up and failed. That is what we need, a large base from which a great success can emerge.'

— ◈ —

Q&A
MANAV GARG

What do you think is a key element for success as an entrepreneur?
Most of the time, in a start-up environment, market changes, things keep changing. You have to be able to execute properly. What you need is perseverance, that dogged determination to succeed. Take the product story in India. People are not available, markets are not yet mature. The only way to do it is to stay very focused, say, 'I want to do it and I am sure I will be able to do it', and then go out there and get it done.

What prompted you to undertake this journey, giving up a high-paying job?
I wanted to create something, to build something. The only way to do that is to take risks. I could have been a good trader all my life and earned a lot of money. But the fun of creating something is very different.

How do you get good ideas, before you can even think about risk taking?
The biggest stumbling block is actually taking risks. I have seen good professionals who can turn around businesses, but they don't want to take risks.

You have to start thinking that you want to change something. Then you will start seeing everything differently. If you see a product say, you won't say, 'Hey, this is good.' You will think, what does this not have? What can I change? The mindset has to come first. Then you won't focus on buying things, for example, you will think, can I change this totally?

What were your initial days like?
I quit my job, I had an idea in my mind about what I wanted to do, so I created a prototype, spoke to experts, industry people. I did that for two years. Entrepreneurship works on a problem statement, which has to be validated. Especially in the enterprise space. You have to build something that solves a client's problems, even if they do not know what they actually want.

Where do you think the product story out of India will go?
The potential is huge. But there has to be a culture of risk taking among all stakeholders. Even VCs (venture capitalists) are not as risk friendly as they should be. As for me, I would rather invest with a new entrepreneur than, say, buy a BMW.

9

Greenko Group Plc

Banking on power
Anil Chalamalasetty

GREENKO GROUP PLC

Founders: Anil Chalamalasetty and Mahesh Kolli

Year of founding: 2006

Headquarters: Hyderabad

Website: www.greenkogroup.com

Area of business: Renewable energy

Revenue: €44.4 million in 2010–11

Profit: €11.4 milliion in 2010–11

Uniqueness

*Greenko is an independent power producer engaged in
clean energy generation through development, acquisition,
construction and operation of hydro, wind, gas, and
biomass power plants. Known for its ability to raise funds
and turn around distressed assets, Greenko aspires
to become a leading Indian renewable energy company.*

By Viswanath Pilla

Everything has happened so fast in the past eight years for Anil Chalamalasetty, chief executive officer and managing director of renewable energy producer Greenko Group Plc., that he finds it difficult sometimes to reconstruct his career as an entrepreneur in a chronological order.

In the interim, the computer scientist by training started companies in information technology (IT), infrastructure, and the environmental sectors in India and the UK before going on to incorporate Greenko in 2006 in Hyderabad with his friend Mahesh Kolli, realizing that his calling lay in renewable energy.

His career as a first-generation entrepreneur began in 2003 when Chalamalasetty and Kolli co-founded an IT services and solutions company called Digi Tele Networks Pvt. Ltd, which built accounting tools for hedge fund managers.

Within a year the duo sold the business and in 2005 started another venture called Lytag Asia, an environmental solutions company that focused on bringing advanced clean energy technologies from Europe to India.

Technologies they worked on included coal gasification and transforming waste from thermal power plants into lightweight building products. Lytag Asia helped Chalamalasetty gain insights on renewable energy, financing, mergers and acquisitions, and carbon trading, which proved valuable in building Greenko.

It was in 2004 that Chalamalasetty and Kolli began developing a business plan in the area of renewable energy.

'Our initial idea was to get into the infrastructure space as it opened up in a big way for the private sector in India,' says Chalamalasetty, now in his late thirties.

'In infra, we narrowed down on the energy vertical given the huge supply-demand gap. Again, in energy, our focus was on renewables as it has fewer entry barriers, sourcing fuel isn't going to be a problem and most importantly it's environment friendly,' explains Chalamalasetty on the logic behind entering the renewable space.

Greenko was finally incorporated in January 2006. Its business plan was to acquire, build, and operate a portfolio of clean energy assets such as biomass, hydro and wind power, and earn revenue from the sale of power to state electricity boards through 15 to 20 year power purchase agreements and through the sale of carbon credits.

Within two months, Greenko raised €6 million from French private equity (PE) firm Aloe Private Equity SAS, which specialises in environmental projects.

To build assets quickly, the company chose the inorganic route. Within six months after raising private equity money, Greenko acquired its first power asset—a small biomass power plant in Andhra Pradesh with a generating capacity of about 7.5 MW.

In the next one year, Greenko went on an acquisition spree. The company bought half-a-dozen small biomass power plants in Andhra Pradesh, Karnataka and Chhattisgarh, taking its total capacity to around 40 MW.

The biomass assets that Greenko bought were either distressed or unable to source feedstock to keep running. 'Our idea was to turn around these troubled assets into operational ones as quickly as possible and make them profitable,' says Chalamalasetty.

More than funds, the challenge was to source feedstock. Greenko secured a proportion of the feedstock locally to reduce transport costs by tying up with local suppliers. The contracts were executed on a seasonal basis whereby prices are typically fixed for a specified duration.

After successfully turning around the biomass power plants, Greenko diversified into hydro-power generation. The company acquired two under-construction mini-hydro power projects of 24.5 MW each on the Nethravathi river in Karnataka.

'Typically, a mini-hydro project requires less initial capital expenditure with shorter construction duration and qualifies for both carbon credits and local tax breaks,' says Chalamalasetty.

In November 2007, Greenko went public by listing its shares on the Alternative Investment Market (AIM) of the London Stock Exchange (LSE). The initial public offering raised $65 million, which was used to invest in new projects and continue buyouts.

'Ours is a capital-intensive business model,' says Chalamalasetty. 'The IPO gave us greater access to a range of projects and AIM enabled us to access capital for the high growth we planned.'

Soon after this, Greenko acquired a 36.8 MW operational plant based on liquid fuel that was to be converted into a 32 MW natural gas plant, with the potential of adding another 85 MW of gas-based generation capacity. The company secured fixed-price gas from the D6 field in the Krishna-Godavari basin for the project.

Two years after the IPO, Greenko raised $46.3 million of private equity in November 2009 from Global Environment Fund and within the next three months, raised $120 million though private placements from Arden Partners, Mirabaud Securities, and TBG Group.

Flush with funds, Greenko diversified into wind energy. It is in the process of setting up 200 MW of wind power capacity in Ratnagiri, Maharashtra. The first phase of 65 MW is expected to be operational by March 2012.

'Given the seasonal nature of renewable energy, we spread our risks geographically and built a diversified portfolio of projects in order to maintain a consistent revenue stream,' Chalamalasetty says.

'For instance, hydro power is seasonal. In the dry season, we will not be in a position to generate any power, but at the same time our wind, gas and biomass plants will help us in generating cash flows,' he explains. 'Similarly, when inflation of feedstock prices may hurt our biomass power plants; wind and hydro will balance it.'

Greenko's operational capacity is 182.6 MW. It wants to take the capacity to 1,000 MW by 2015. Greenko has already tied up finances for 300 MW under development.

It has 14 operating projects and 10 projects under construction across various locations, some as distant as Sikkim and Nepal.

'Growth comes easy, but managing and sustaining it is a huge challenge,' says Chalamalasetty.

In October 2011, the company raised $50 million from GE Energy Financial Services for a subsidiary called Greenko Wind Project Pvt. Ltd. The GE investment will support the development of 500 MW of wind projects. In December 2011, Greenko raised another $70 million from Standard Chartered Plc.

Chalamalasetty was born in the coastal town of Machilipatnam in Andhra Pradesh to a physician father and homemaker mother. A graduate in computer science, Chalamalasetty received a master's degree from North West University in the UK, where he also worked for a couple of companies before turning entrepreneur.

When he isn't immersed in work, Chalamalasetty spends time with his two children. He plays badminton, spends time on the golf course, and tries his hand at flying.

Chalamalasetty says the Greenko growth story wouldn't have happened if not for the active support he received from business partner Kolli, who is president and joint managing director.

'We both disagree on numerous occasions, but that brings a different perspective which helps the business ultimately,' Chalamalasetty says.

— ◆ —

Q&A
ANIL CHALAMALASETTY

What motivated you to become an entrepreneur?
By 2001, I was leading quite a comfortable life, both professionally and personally.
But I wanted to do something exciting. I wanted to become an entrepreneur, and my brother, who was into business by then, encouraged me.

Who is your role model?
I can't name one role model in particular. As a person I always keep learning. Whenever I come across someone who is inspiring, I will try to learn from them.

How did you get the idea of entering the renewable energy space?
India, to sustain its energy security, needs to de-risk itself from fossil fuels. It's a no-brainer that globally coal and gasoline prices are skyrocketing and energy prices also will go in the same direction. India has enormous renewable resources to tap and it will be more economical to implement renewable projects here. India is 30 per cent cheaper than the rest of the world to set up a renewable energy project. We took that arbitrage and got good value out of it.

What were your challenges?
Our asset portfolio is spread across different states, some as remote as Sikkim, so we come across different socio-cultural-political types of people. Dealing with them is a challenge but a huge learning experience. Also, in power projects, you have to deal with the bureaucracy. Given the strong corporate governance practices we follow, we maintain transparency in all our dealings with the bureaucracy and try to avoid any shady dealings.

What qualities helped you become a successful entrepreneur?
It all boils down to hard work. In the last five years, I have put in work that is equivalent to 20 years. A lot of hard work, determination, and good team effort is what helped us to build such a diversified class of assets.

What is your advice to upcoming entrepreneurs?
I see a business opportunity everywhere. Especially in India, we have enormous opportunities. Before starting a business now, you need to figure out how you bring value addition to the existing product or process. And how do you replicate that value addition and how do you scale it. To develop the value addition into a marketable product or service you need to have discipline, good governance practices, and hard work. Access to capital, access to technologies, and aligning your business to global standards also plays a key role.

10

Johnson Lifts

Climbing the ladder of success
John K. John

JOHNSON LIFTS

Founder: John K. John

Year of founding: 1970

Headquarters: Chennai

Website: www.johnsonliftsltd.com

Area of business: Elevators and escalators manufacturing

Revenue: ₹700 crore in 2010–11

Profit: Not disclosed

Uniqueness

In the elevator and escalator space, Johnson Lifts has an early mover advantage in manufacturing escalators and plans to venture into travelators. To build its brand further the company will move into high-end, high-speed lifts in the coming years.

By S. Bridget Leena

As India opened up its economy in 1991, some domestic companies considered liberalization a bane as it would usher in international competition. Not Johnson Lifts Ltd, which saw in it a ticket for growth.

In the technology-intensive field of elevators, India's then closed economy was barely conducive to a business dependent on overseas research and development. Travelling abroad to access new technologies and knowhow required an endorsement from the central bank for foreign exchange and often, a formal invitation from an overseas company or organizer.

'Liberalization made it easier to travel abroad to see the latest technology and also attend international elevator exhibitions so we know how the industry was progressing and where we stood,' says John K. John, chairman and managing director.

Until 1990, the firm had taken two decades to produce 1,000 lifts. In the years immediately after liberalization, the company made 100 lifts a year and by the end of that decade had progressed to 1,000 a year. It makes 7,000 lifts a year today.

The maker of lifts and escalators began its life as a small-scale enterprise in north Chennai's Vysarpadi industrial estate 40 years ago. The seeds of the business were sown by John's father A.J. John, who at age of 40 quit his job with Best & Co., a lift company, and started his own elevator maintenance firm in 1963. The company progressed to installation of lifts and finally began making elevators in 1970, competing with foreign firms that boasted of more advanced technologies.

Elevator companies at the time made the various parts they required in-house as sourcing components from other firms was unheard of. This, obviously, limited the number of lifts that could be made and business was slow.

Still, John's father recognized the potential of the business and didn't give up on setting the stage for his son. 'My dad used to discuss elevators at home while having lunch or dinner,' says the soft-spoken John.

The now salt and pepper-haired chairman began imbibing the 'nuts and bolts' of the elevator business as a young boy. The dining table talk drilled into him the importance of after-sales service. 'Without maintenance there is no business,' John learnt.

Soon after he graduated from the Maulana Azad National Institute of Technology in Bhopal, he joined the family business in 1978 as a technician at a salary of ₹350 a month. He didn't get to pocket the entire money; his father would deduct ₹150 from the pay cheque. John didn't know it then, but his father would use the money to buy shares in his son's name when Johnson Lifts was made a private limited company in 1981.

Taking over the reins didn't come without conditions either. The elder John insisted his son complete his electronic engineering course to be clued into the workings of the equipment the company makes.

One of the toughest challenges the business has faced since inception was competition from multinational companies. To overcome its disadvantage in technology, Johnson Lifts decided to set benchmarks in the market in terms of product quality and process. 'For example, our unique selling proposition was that we looked into a customer complaint the same day it was received, which was unheard of 30 years ago,' John says.

That attitude coupled with rapid urbanization catalyzed the company's growth in the previous decade. From being confined to southern states, Johnson Lifts went pan-India in 1999. Today, the company has a 20 per cent share in the Indian market, holding the No.1 position in the southern states of Kerala, Tamil Nadu, Karnataka, and Andhra Pradesh.

Johnson had to adapt quickly to make the climb.

A bulk of Johnson Lifts' business was from residential apartments. In 2000, as commercial construction and government development projects gained pace, elevator companies could often make a pitch only if they offered escalators in the package.

Recognizing the gap, John forged a partnership with Chinese escalator maker SJEC Corp. that year and formed a consortium to supply the devices for the second phase of the Delhi Metro project. Johnson Lifts has subsequently won Metro projects in Bangalore and Chennai as well.

In a sense, the Chinese collaboration was merely a trading deal as the escalators were imported but it developed in John an itch to begin manufacturing them. He went on to set up the country's only escalator manufacturing plant at Oragadam near Chennai, inaugurated last year. The tie up with the Chinese company is now only for technology transfer.

The Chennai-based company is also spreading overseas through wholly owned subsidiaries. In 2006, it set up operations in Sri Lanka and Nepal. 'I was testing waters as to how we can do things outside the country,' says John.

But it is a delicate balance to manage expansion and customer satisfaction in the elevator business involving three processes—supply,

71

installation, and after-sales service. While manufacturing elevators and escalators may seem complicated enough, the real challenge is to doggedly address customer complaints.

'We need to be careful while expanding and replicating the same process elsewhere,' John explains.

And in an era of rising costs, keeping a tight hold on spending too is imperative.

'Beginning of 2008, we were hit hard by rising metal prices since it takes one-and-half years from order to execution of the project and it is tough to estimate such a rise,' John says. But such uncertainties can be tackled if the business is inherently prudent. 'We are a conservative company. If we have ₹100 in the pocket we would think of spending ₹10 and not borrow for expansion.'

Q&A
JOHN K. JOHN

Who are the people most responsible for the success of Johnson Lifts?

First, my father A.J. John, who started this company. My dad envisaged the growth of the elevator industry when demand for lifts was a handful in the 1960s. In the initial years of financial difficulty, when some other company offered to buy out Johnson Lifts, my dad stuck to his conviction and vision. Subsequently, it goes to team work. A.V. Thomas, joint managing director and my brother-in-law, who oversees manufacturing, and K. Subramanium, an expert in elevators, and me.

How was the brand Johnson Lifts created without television or print advertisements?

It is largely due to the after-sales service we offer. As a policy, we maintain only Johnson Lifts. We made a rough estimate that at least a million people use our lifts every day. Most people would see the name of elevator when they travel. This is the safest mode of transportation.

What is the primary requisite while pitching for government projects?

Being in business we may be tempted to provide a better alternative for a specific requirement, say a motor design, but it is important to stick to the specification of the tender proposal.

Where do you think Johnson Lifts is yet to make a mark? What are your plans for the future?

I would like to see us being present in the high-end market, particularly in five-star hotels, which creates value addition for the brand. We would like to expand to travelators, which is still a very small market in India with a handful demand. We have got a licence to manufacture them in the country but will wait for foreign direct investment in retail to grow and then set up a facility.

(Travelators are moving walkways installed at facilities such as airports.)

What advice do you have for aspiring entrepreneurs?

Do not concentrate on profit and loss when you start out but focus on work, and profits will automatically follow suit. One should be waiting for Sunday to get over and be happy to start work on a Monday morning. This is the kind of drive one should have to succeed.

11

Manappuram Group

Midas touch
V.P. Nandakumar

MANAPPURAM GROUP

Founder: V.C. Padmanabhan
Year of founding: 1949
Headquarters: Thrissur
Website: www.manappuram.com
Area of business: Gold loans, vehicle loans,
asset finance, foreign exchange, money transfer,
gold retail, and healthcare.
Revenue: ₹1,500 crore in 2010–11
Profit: ₹287 crore in 2010–11

Uniqueness

*Scaling up a finance business, given tight Indian banking
regulations, is always difficult. But Nandakumar,
a pioneer in gold loan financing, looked beyond
the obvious and made accessible the otherwise
mundane pawn-broking business.*

By Amritha Venketakrishnan

For someone who lost out on a career as a doctor, V.P. Nandakumar seems at peace with the accident that landed him in the ₹1,500 crore group that is credited with bringing gold loan financing to the forefront.

His father, V.C. Padmanabhan, had earned a reputation running a small-scale money lending business that he started six decades ago.

For Nandakumar, growing up in Valapad, a small coastal village in Thrissur, Kerala, getting involved in the family business was inevitable. 'I used to be there after school to help out. So that created some interest for me,' he recalls.

The zoology graduate, who failed the qualifying exam for a medical course by a slender margin, signed on as a bank officer for Nedungadi Bank without an inkling of finance. 'The terms credit and debit were foreign to me. I even thought of quitting after a while,' says Nandakumar. 'But I wanted to understand the business and wrote the exam to qualify as a banker.'

In 1986, his father's terminal illness brought him to a crossroads, where he had to choose between his family business and the bank job. In the end, it came down to potential. Having spent the previous three years in his village, he had seen demand swell for his family business, with people queuing up with their deposits only to be turned away by his father's self-imposed limits.

'I had a great launching pad as my father had already done the hard work of gaining the trust and goodwill of the people. Even today, it remains my greatest capital,' says the 57-year-old.

Nandakumar's appetite to grow the business saw him do away with his father's conservative limits and take the ₹25 lakh loan book to ₹10-12 crore in five years. 'From the very first day, my thought was to expand the business,' he says.

He went one step further and in 1992 entered vehicle financing with Manappuram General Finance and Leasing Ltd to supplement his capital needs, his focus wavering from the core gold loan business. Soon, disaster struck in the late 1990s, as the central bank's stringent regulations to curb the unhealthy practices stemming from the rapid growth in this sector put a crimp on deposits for non-banking financial companies, or NBFCs. The new norms brought in revised requirements of capital-asset ratios that tightened conditions. Many NBFCs folded. Nandakumar was forced to take a hard look at his own asset-liability mismatch.

'Like they say, necessity is the mother of invention. Circumstances forced me to innovate,' he says. He then brought the lucrative gold loan business under the ambit of the main company, a move that proved a game changer for people looking for transparent, independent financing.

'Gold loans have a very short lifespan and on average have a life of four months,' he says. As a result, he could get his returns much faster, with the added advantage of a solid, non-risky collateral in the bag, unlike, for instance, in vehicle financing, which has a longer gestation period that can create liquidity problems when depositors demand their money back.

Nandakumar stayed relentless in his pursuit to expand the company. Frustrated by his inability to raise funds quickly from banks, he decided to list the company on the stock exchanges in 1995.

This was no mean feat, as he had to do some fast talking to local businessmen and customers in his village to convert their deposits to shares and convince them to take the plunge with him, as government regulations dictated that the company must have a minimum capital of ₹3 crore to go public.

'It was an emotionally trying time for me as some of my close associates even stopped talking to me because they thought this was similar to me approaching them for a donation,' says Nandakumar. 'I had to personally guarantee to buy back their shares with interest if things went wrong.'

He did exactly that when share prices plummeted soon after it was listed and didn't stabilize for nearly a year, a risky move that only made him determined to focus on the business fundamentals, even as some professional directors went on to abandon what they perceived to be a sinking ship.

Perseverance, he says is a trait every entrepreneur must imbibe. 'In business, you will have more adversity than achievements,' says the Kerala-based entrepreneur. 'In football, there are many players, but only a select few are sharp shooters. This is because they have the focus required to achieve the goal.'

Although the company gained ground, there was no cash for the planned massive expansion. The central bank's guidelines on funding available to NBFCs was meant that he was not able to produce the security required for the sizable loans. But white-knight investor ICICI Bank Ltd's suggestion to securitize the gold loans in 2005 was a counter-intuitive strategy that worked. The gold loans were transferred to ICICI's books and with that Manappuram was able to secure a much needed infusion of ₹100 crore to fuel its growth.

But ICICI failed to get regulatory approval for a second round of funding in 2006, leaving Manappuram, which was riding the expansion wave and expecting another ₹1,000 crore in funding, in the lurch.

'We had already opened so many branches in hopes that these funds will come in. Closing down the branches also affects the credibility. So I had to look out for an alternative source,' Nandakumar says.

Singapore-based NBFC Temasek Holdings's Indian subsidiary Fullerton was looking to ramp up its operations and recognised the potential gold mine in Manappuram. Fullerton India bought Manappuram's gold loan portfolio for ₹500 crore. Soon, international private equity investors including US-based Sequoia Capital lined up to put their money in the growing business, which helped tide over capital adequacy difficulties.

'Many smaller companies benefited from this model as they started emulating it for smaller capital needs of maybe ₹25 crore,' says Nandakumar.

But the 2009 global financial meltdown brought on speed bumps for one of his key investors, Fullerton India, which, facing liquidity issues, called in its loan and had him scrambling to repay over half of the loan book in a matter of four months.

Nandakumar, though, is not one to dwell in the past as he now plans to go full throttle selling gold jewellery to retail customers. 'With over 25 years of experience in gold loans, I feel a retail venture will be successful given our understanding of risks,' he says.

With his proven eye for high-potential businesses, Nandakumar has set the ball rolling to take a new line of affordable healthcare centres, branded MAcare, to South Indian destinations.

What started as a one-branch, pawn shop in Kerala is today present in 23 states through 2,800 offices, with nearly ₹12,000 crore of assets under management. Soon, Manappuram Finance will be seen in international destinations in Asia through joint ventures with local banks.

'When I took up the family business, I wanted to make good on what I had lost (his bank job). My ambition is to excel in all areas of business I have entered into,' says Nandakumar.

— ◈ —

Q&A
V.P. NANDAKUMAR

You were one of the first to advertise gold loans. Tell us about that.
Advertising for gold loans was unheard of back then. Usually banks and financiers advertise a higher rate of interest for deposits and not their loans. I had only one branch, where deposits were pouring in and I was growing 100-200% without being able to lend. I had plenty of money with me, so I had to advertise loans.

Tell us about your experience as a banker in the early days.
Initially, I was not familiar with finance and it used to irritate me to a point where I even thought of quitting. But my manager convinced me to stick on and soon I applied for a certificate course as a banker and qualified for it within a year of joining. This helped me get noticed by the bank. I travelled extensively, worked at the headquarters on proposals, where I helped small traders get working capital loans. The company even consulted me as an expert on gold jewellery. So, these experiences did help me understand the workings of a corporate body.

Tell us how you chanced upon the idea of securitizing the loans when it wasn't a common practice to get funding back then?
Again, like a bolt from the blue, K.V. Kamath became the chairman of the new generation ICICI Bank. My team worked with ICICI executives to come up with a product that was not a loan. This was necessary because to get a ₹100 crore loan in Indian banking you will need to offer collateral that is double the size of the loan.

Though the product (securitization) was already available in the market, no one had sought to do it on such a large scale. So then Manappuram's loan book was transferred to ICICI's books with the condition that we manage and collect the loans for them and the ₹100-crore infusion went on to fund our expansion.

What were some of the problems you faced along the way?
Back then, I had taken the unconventional route, using only professionals in a family business so I could get guidance from them. I could not afford to employ chartered accountants and company secretaries and still show a profit record. So, for over 15 years, I sacrificed my salary as the chief executive and paid them from my own pocket.

12

MedPlus Health Services Pvt. Ltd

Pharma profits
Madhukar Gangadi

MEDPLUS HEALTH SERVICES PVT. LTD

Founder: Madhukar Gangadi
Year of founding: 2006
Headquarters: Hyderabad
Website: www.medplusindia.com
Area of business: Pharmacy retail
Revenue: Not disclosed
Profit: Not disclosed

Uniqueness

MedPlus is India's second-biggest and fastest-growing organized pharmacy retail chain with 1,000-plus stores across six states. MedPlus, with its supply chain efficiency, is able to bring down medicine prices by 10% and guarantees genuine drugs, offering quality storage, a wide choice of brands and free home delivery.

By Viswanath Pilla

Madhukar Gangadi is a physician by training, but his heart was always in business. So it came as no surprise when he chose to become a particle board distributor in Hyderabad after graduating with an MBBS degree from Kurnool Medical College in Andhra Pradesh instead of practising medicine.

After that came a fleeting stint in information technology (IT) services before Gangadi, in 1998, moved to the US. He became a partner in an IT company where he spent a while before starting his own consulting firm, Tech Nation Software Consulting Inc., in South Dakota.

To hone his management skills, Gangadi went to the Wharton School of the University of Pennsylvania for an MBA programme in healthcare management. It was at the B-school that the concept of MedPlus, today India's second-largest organized pharma retail chain, took shape.

'I was writing a small business plan for a company—a group purchasing organization,' Gangadi, founder and chief executive officer of MedPlus Health Services Pvt. Ltd, recollects.

A group purchasing organization (GPO) is an entity that leverages the buying power of a group of businesses to obtain discounts from vendors. In the US, hospitals make purchases through a GPO to take advantage of the collective buying power of its members.

'I was looking at the feasibility of such an organization in India,' Gangadi says.

In the course of his research on the subject, Gangadi found that supply chain inefficiencies inflated the price of drugs in India and, at the same time, customers had to contend with the problem of fake medicines.

'I saw a World Health Organization report which said that 30 per cent of all fake drugs in the world were made in India, so that made me think. If there was a company out there which could sell products that were guaranteed as genuine, customers should automatically come—that was the premise on which I started the company.'

To execute his business plan, Gangadi raised the equivalent of ₹2.25 crore from his family and friends in the US. MedPlus opened its first store in February 2006 in Hyderabad and took the number to 50 across Hyderabad and Bangalore in a rapid ramp-up.

The model of MedPlus was simple: It established a central warehouse around which it put up as many stores as possible. The cost of the warehouse was amortized across the stores. The company used technology extensively for better supply chain management and to network the stores and warehouses.

To reduce real estate costs, MedPlus set up its stores in city bylanes and ensured that their size didn't exceed 300 sq.ft.

Gangadi raised around ₹6.75 crore more from family and friends to invest on network expansion, to set up warehouses and strengthen the supply chain.

The advantages of bulk buying, high volume sales, supply-chain efficiencies, and optimal operational costs helped MedPlus offer a 10 per cent outright discount to customers.

With MedPlus winning popularity among customers, local retail pharmacy associations dominated by unorganized family run drug stores began pushing back against it.

'They tried to block our entry,' says Gangadi. 'They went to the drug inspectors out there and made them delay the whole licensing process. They used to go to the local distributor associations and tell them not to supply to us. They used to threaten distributors with cutting of their own business, meaning if the distributor supplied to us, he will lose the business of the other 2,000-3,000 stores in that town.'

Despite such hurdles, MedPlus managed to keep its stores running by sourcing drugs from different locations. Soon enough, the opposition died down.

'Luckily for us, we managed to overcome that because the industry itself is very fragmented. If people in Hyderabad stopped supplying to us, we got supplies from distributors in Vizag, Vijayawada, or Bangalore,' Gangadi explains. 'After a while people realized that there is no point in stopping supplies (to us), and they relented.'

Over the next few years, MedPlus went on expanding its pharmacy stores. Today, it has 1,000-plus stores concentrated around metro cities in six states and recently added the National Capital Region, where it has opened 34 outlets.

Typically, a store requires ₹15-20 lakh of investment and it takes on average a year for it to break even. Some 90 per cent of MedPlus stores have reached the break-even stage. The company had sales of around ₹460 crore in the fiscal year ended 31 March, 2011. It expects revenue to increase to ₹650 crore this fiscal year. With scale came new challenges. MedPlus had to shutter its stores in two states.

'Pharmacy retail is easier to start with if you just want to do 100 stores in just one location,' Gangadi explains. 'Only when you start doing multi-location (business) and add hundreds of stores, do you start seeing the problems of management bandwidth, and very quickly you lose control of the business and things start falling apart.'

MedPlus learnt its lessons, ensuring tighter controls on inventory and constantly auditing and monitoring store operations.

The pharmacy retail market in India is worth ₹52,000 crore, of which organised retail accounts for just 5 per cent. Going forward, Gangadi says the MedPlus plan is to gain 10 per cent of the total Indian pharmacy retail market.

'Organized retail is going to grow,' says Gangadi, who in his spare time plays golf, reads books, and watches movies.

MedPlus has benefited all stakeholders, he says. Customers get access to genuine medicines at a discount, pharma companies can use the chain's outlets to introduce new products, and distributors get a lot more business from a single source without having to run from shop to shop. Even pharmacists, who struggled to make ₹5,000 a month, are earning double that now, he says.

Gangadi plans to tap the potential of the Internet more aggressively to increase sales. Going beyond MedPlus, Gangadi runs a menswear retail chain called Cornerstone, which he recently rebranded as My Smart Shop. He is currently in the process of streamlining that business.

Q&A
MADHUKAR GANGADI

What motivated you to become an entrepreneur?

I have always been an entrepreneur. Ever since I graduated from medical college in 1991, I have been in business. I came out of school and got into business. One of the first things which I did was become a distributor for a product that was newly launched in India at that point of time. It was called New Wood. From there on to doing plywood, timber, IT services, it has been a long haul—most of it has been spent in business.

Who were your role models?

Honestly, on the business side, I haven't really had a role model. But over the years I have been reading a lot... about Sam Walton (founder of Wal-Mart Stores Inc.) and a bunch of different leaders out there. Jack Welch (former chairman and chief executive officer of General Electric Co.), Richard Branson (Virgin Atlantic). But I wouldn't say any one of them was my role model. It's just that some of my ideas got validated, I would say. It did not feel strange for me to get out of the medical profession and go into business.

What's your approach to entrepreneurship?

I have always been excited by new ideas. You go through life looking at various things out there and when you see the inefficiency of something out there or when you see an arbitrage opportunity, instantly think... there could be something for a businessman to go and maybe do this process a little bit more differently and a little bit more efficiently. At least for me I have gone through life evaluating different things, constantly looking to see if there is a way in which it could be done better. Apart from MedPlus, my other businesses also address similar kind of problems in inventory and everything else.

The style I would say is one of discovering an opportunity out there and then validating it really quickly and going out there and trying to implement it.

Very entrepreneurial, I would say, doing everything from scratch, getting involved right from the business plan to signing the lease agreements to hiring the first employee, getting the first outlet together, getting the first business prototype together and everything else.

Any key learnings?

Nothing is ever perfect when you start. You start off the business thinking that you will do something and it usually ends up being something else. But if you are on the case 24x7, then you can make small changes and corrections (that are) necessary. Being able to adapt constantly and perfecting it to the needs of the business is what makes the entire plan successful. MedPlus has been pretty much a planned thing—whatever we thought we would actually implement has happened with a few minor changes here and there.

What advice would you give potential and upcoming entrepreneurs?

For me at least, I always have done whatever I wanted to do. So I never let either the current situation or my past education stand in the way of what I actually wanted to do or where I saw the opportunity. So the best advice to a potential businessman is: Do what you like best doing, don't do it just because you hate working for someone else, or don't do it just because you want to make a lot of money. If you like what you are doing, you do a lot of it, and you do it well—you will automatically make the money. There is a lot of opportunity out there, but don't just do it just because you think, 'Hey, you know what, I worked for long enough for someone else and now I'll be my own boss.' That is not the way and that's not the reason you want to do it. The only reason you want to do it is only if you see a fantastic opportunity out there and you feel strongly enough to throw away your current job or throw away everything you like and go and pursue it. In that case you'll be successful because then you would be thinking and dreaming of that 24x7.

— ◈ —

13

Mu Sigma

Numbers worth crunching
Dhiraj C. Rajaram

MU SIGMA

Founder: Dhiraj C. Rajaram
Year of founding: December 2004
Headquarters: Ilinois, US
Website: www.mu-sigma.com
Area of business: Decision sciences and analytics services
Revenue: Not disclosed
Profit: Not disclosed

Uniqueness

After working with various business analytics units at Booz Allen Hamilton (now known as Booz & Co.), Dhiraj C. Rajaram realized that neither business consultancies nor information technology firms were bringing applied mathematics to the table in helping companies address their problems and improve organizational efficiency. Today, Mu Sigma has an in-house training programme where new recruits are put through a rigorous training programme in consulting principles, applied math, and technology.

By Byravee Iyer

Dhiraj C. Rajaram was tipped to become a partner at Booz and Co. when he chucked his job to start Mu Sigma Inc. in 2004. His is a 'decision sciences' company that works with clients to help solve business problems using data analysis.

Having received an MBA degree from the University of Chicago Booth School of Business after training to be an engineer, Rajaram was working with various business analytics units at Booz when he realized a need for the company he went on to found.

Neither business consultancies nor information technology firms were bringing applied mathematics to the table in helping companies address their problems and improve organizational efficiency, says Rajaram, now 36.

At the time, data was doubling every 18 months, the cost of computer memory was declining and computing power was increasing. These trends indicated that companies needed a combination of math, business consulting, and technology to make better decisions on a consistent basis, Rajaram says.

So with a business plan in mind, Rajaram, married and with a child, quit his job, sold his house, and moved into a 600-sq.ft. one-bedroom apartment. He put all his money into Mu Sigma.

Business was slow to begin with. Hiring talent was the biggest problem.

'I was 28 and not somebody who people would give up their careers for,' he smiles. He must have interviewed close to seventy people, some of whom promised to join him later; others flatly refused.

Luckily for Rajaram, he was unabashed about asking for help, so much so that he refers to himself as the chief apologetic officer of his company.

After around eighty pitches to various companies, Mu Sigma got its first client and a big one at that—Microsoft Corp. Prior to the launch of Microsoft's operating system Vista, executives at Mu Sigma were coming up with a predictive modeling project that helped the software maker with the final design plan. It also helped Microsoft determine what customers to focus on.

'We worked very hard to make sure Microsoft was happy,' recalls Rajaram.

With Microsoft as a client, business became easier. Pharmaceutical giant Pfizer Inc., fast food chain McDonald's Corp., marketing communications company McCann Worldgroup, and computer maker Dell Inc. also became clients. Today, the data company counts seventy five Fortune 500 companies among its customers.

The sudden upsurge of interest in data-driven analtyical expertise won over investors as well. First to jump onto the bandwagon was Angel Investors, shelling out ₹7.2 crore for an undisclosed stake in the company.

Other institutional investors such as Accel, FTVetures, Helion Ventures and, more recently, Sequoia Capital also chipped in.

Here, Rajaram reveals his approach towards investors. 'Never part with your equity easily, hold on to as much stock as possible,' says the entrepreneur, who still owns a majority stake in the company.

Mu Sigma operates on a dual business model—information technology and applied math, and consulting and applied math.

While Rajaram is tight-lipped about revenue numbers, he says clients pay him on a service basis.

Intellectual property is a lucrative income avenue. So far, the analytics company has about 20 intellectual assets, including workbench, marketing optimization, and fraud analysis tools.

This, Rajaram says, has helped the company grow 40 per cent every year for the past five years. Its headcount has increased from 150 employees in 2007 to about 1,500, and it has offices in the US, the UK, and India. The company is also looking to expand in Europe, Australia, West Asia, and South Africa.

But there are big competitors stepping into its space—International Business Machines Corp., Accenture Inc., and Infosys Ltd are all building analytical tools. Even business consulting firms such as Booz, AT Kearney, and McKinsey & Co. are getting into data-driven analytics on a project-to-project basis. There are also the erstwhile pure-play research companies such as Nielsen Holdings NV and IMS Research that are hoping to make their mark here, not to mention smaller boutique shops.

Ask Rajaram about the competition from deep-pocketed rivals, and he laughs it off. 'Consulting is overpriced and not data-driven, and IT companies are usually not very responsive,' he says. 'IBM and the rest are doing 15-20 other things, and for them to think innovatively isn't going to be easy.'

Besides, Mu Sigma offers the cost advantage of outsourced services—a data analyst in India is likely to be paid far less than his American counterpart.

That apart, there are other challenges Rajaram has to contend with. Talent remains an issue for Mu Sigma. A company like his requires cross-functional skills comprising applied mathematics, technology, and domain expertise. And that is increasingly hard to come by. Which is why he's forced to create this talent.

Today, MuSigma has an in-house training programme called Mu Sigma University at which new recruits are put through a rigorous training programme in consulting principles, applied math, and technology.

Investing in talented mathematicians is going to pay off. A report by McKinsey Global Institute estimates that by 2018 there will be demand for at least 200,000 data scientists in the US alone.

The accolades have, meanwhile, been pouring in for Mu Sigma. INC magazine has named it one of the fastest growing entrepreneurial businesses in the world with a three-year growth rate of 1,500 per cent. Mu Sigma was also ranked No. 1 in Datamonitor's annual KPO, or knowledge process outsourcing, rankings ahead of IBM, Accenture, Capgemini, and Infosys.

Those are numbers worth crunching.

Q&A
DHIRAJ C. RAJARAM

What prompted you to start a company?
Mu Sigma started in December 2004; the vision for the company was to help organizations institutionalize the use of data-driven decision making. We are a decision sciences company and the company got started when I saw the need for decision sciences to be a big problem that needed to be solved. Data was doubling every 18 months, the cost of memory was getting cheaper, computing power was increasing—all of these things were trends that indicated that companies needed a combination of math, business, and technology to help make better decisions on a consistent basis. I never wanted to be an entrepreneur. I was working at Booz Allen Hamilton—now Booz and Company. I loved my job, was doing well there and I even wanted to be a partner when we basically saw this opportunity. I talked about this to everyone, and the only thing was to solve this problem—how I was going to do it was not in my mind. Starting a company happened to be a means to that end.

Quitting your job at that point of your career, how scary was it?
I think there was always a little bit of fear. It's about somehow figuring out a way to deal with that fear. Family does help but it's a very lonely world.

When did you reach the inflection point?
The first few months were very, very lonely. But I think that was the best thing that happened to me because on a consistent basis I was subject to a good amount of failure, which enabled me to think of every reason why the company would fail, every possible objection an employee or customer would raise, and what one needs to do to handle that. And that was a gift. Microsoft eventually gave us a break. They understood we were small and were very magnanimous... And we never looked back after that.

How vulnerable is a business like yours to an economic slowdown?
We're absolutely vulnerable. But I'm excited about a downturn as much as I am about an upturn. A downturn tests you. All great companies have been built in downturns. Google was built when the Internet bubble

94

burst. *It's a good test. You have to go through one. It's a good time for us to go through that as it will separate the men from the boys and it'll show that we're here for the long run. There's another reason—the business of decision sciences is always there. During upturns they make decisions orienting towards growth. Now it'll be optimization, cost savings, and de-risking. As long as decision making is needed we're in good shape.*

What's one mistake you'd advise other entrepreneurs not to repeat?

Get legal counsel. Entrepreneurs tend to be frugal in the first few years, and you don't want to spend money on a lawyer. Also, don't ever carry the burden of being the smartest person in the room.

— ◆ —

14

Neuland Laboratories Ltd

Entrepreneurial ingredients
Davuluri Rama Mohan Rao

NEULAND LABORATORIES LTD

Founder: Davuluri Rama Mohan Rao

Year of founding: 1984

Headquarters: Hyderabad

Website: www.neulandlabs.com

Area of business: API manufacturing and contract
research

Revenue: ₹397.95 crore in 2010–11

Profit: ₹5.27 crore in 2010–11

Uniqueness

*Neuland has carved a niche for itself as a quality supplier
of active pharmaceutical ingredients. The company is a
seasoned player in highly regulated markets like the US
and Europe, with proven manufacturing capabilities. It
has built a large R&D centre to support its ambitious
plan to become an end-to-end service provider for the
pharmaceutical industry.*

By Viswanath Pilla

A dusty, potholed road, an unusual odour, and a scattering of
industrial buildings—some dilapidated and some turned into
warehouses—welcome you to Bonthapally's industrial development
area, some 40 km from Hyderabad. The sick units are testament
to a bulk drug dream that died early. One unit stands tall amid the
ruins—the active pharmaceutical ingredient (API) facility of Neuland
Laboratories Ltd. A short distance from the plant is a state-of-the-art
research and development laboratory.

Many entrepreneurs in Hyderabad jumped onto the API
bandwagon in the 1980s to make a quick buck. Only a few, like
Davuluri Rama Mohan Rao, who were committed to quality and
good governance practices, survived the intense competition and a
price-sensitive market.

Neuland's D.R. Rao, as he is known, is a first-generation entrepreneur from a middle class family in Kakinada in Andhra Pradesh. His father was an officer in the customs and central excise department, a job that entailed moving to different parts of the country. Rao travelled along. He would eventually acquire a degree in organic chemistry from the Indian Institute of Technology, Kharagpur, and a doctorate in the same subject from the University of Notre Dame in the US.

For about 10 years, before he began his entrepreneurial innings, Rao was a researcher at the Indian Institute of Science, Bangalore, and later held positions in research, production, and quality assurance at Glaxo India.

'With my experience and knowledge in the pharmaceutical industry for about a decade, and interactions I had with other entrepreneurs, by the early 1980s I felt that even I could be a successful entrepreneur in the pharmaceutical industry,' says Rao.

With his penchant for science and innovation, he named his company after Belgian scientist Julius Arthur Nieuland, inventor of synthetic rubber and an alumnus of the University of Notre Dame.

Rao began with seed capital of ₹1 crore, largely met through grants and loans from the government and financial institutions. He and his friends added equity contributions.

Neuland commenced commercial production of salbutamol sulphate and its intermediates in June 1986 from the Bonthapally plant, which can manufacture 1.2 tonnes a year. Salbutamol sulphate is an active ingredient in drugs used to manage conditions such as asthma and chronic obstructive pulmonary disease.

Neuland grew its API portfolio and manufacturing capacities through the early 1990s, adding anti-asthmatic ingredient terbutaline sulphate, anti-hypertension labetalol hydrochloride, and antibiotic ciprofloxacin.

The company listed its shares on stock exchanges in 1994, raising ₹7.8 crore in an initial public offering that was oversubscribed seventy times. Rao used the money to set up a second API facility, in Pashamylaram on the outskirts of Hyderabad, investing a total of ₹15.7 crore.

The new facility allowed him to add cardiovascular ingredient enalapril, anti-ulcer ranitidine hydrochloride, and antibiotics such as norfloxacin, ofloxacin, and pefloxacin to Neuland's APIs portfolio.

Rao soon found the domestic market crowded with too many competitors. Margins were under pressure and he wasn't sure if he would be able to sustain the business. The mid-1990s turned out to be a defining moment.

'If we have to survive as an organization, we must look towards the regulatory markets of the US and Europe,' says Rao, chairman and managing director, recalling his decision that shaped the company's future over the next decade and a half.

Neuland began building systems and processes in tune with the stringent requirements of these foreign markets. Within three years of the public listing, the company got the US drug regulator's approval for its flagship product salbutamol sulphate.

Then in 1999, Neuland got a string of regulatory approvals for its major products and facilities from the US Food and Drug Administration. Rao's decision to enter regulatory markets started to yield results by 2003—40 per cent of the company revenue was from regulated markets.

'My idea of entrepreneurship is whatever we do, we have to do better than others. Then, only then, can we survive as entrepreneurs,' Rao says.

Neuland, which started with 40 employees, now has close to 1,000 people on its rolls. It has nearly 700 customers in 82 countries, generating about 80 per cent of its revenue through exports. And its product portfolio spans a mix of APIs in eight therapeutic categories.

Rao took Neuland on an expansion spree three years ago. The company invested ₹112.6 crore on scaling its manufacturing facilities and ventured into contract research to widen its revenue stream. It invested ₹33.8 crore in a 40,000 sq.ft. state-of-the-art R&D centre in 2008. The company also entered the complex peptide API space

99

and plans to launch four products in the second half of the next financial year.

But Rao, now 67, can't afford to rest on its laurels. Many analysts point out that though Neuland has been around for nearly three decades, several newer API companies, including Divis Laboratories Ltd and Aurobindo Pharma Ltd, have overtaken it in terms of growth and market size.

'We made some mistakes,' concedes Rao. 'We were not shrewd at investing. It's part of learning but we never took short cuts for growth. Overall, I am glad that we laid a strong foundation for the company based on sound professional values.'

Rao continues to be the guiding force of the company but the day-to-day operations are handled by his sons, chief executive Davaluri Sucheth Rao and Davaluri Saharsh Rao, who oversee the contract research business.

'My sons have passion for the business. Sucheth was instrumental in setting up the R&D centre and expansion of API business; Saharsh is passionate about business development and strategy. Under them, the company has an exciting future ahead,' Rao says.

Q&A
DAVULURI RAMA MOHAN RAO

What inspired you to become an entrepreneur?
Right from my childhood days I was interested in chemistry. Knowingly or unknowingly, that helped me in my profession. I travelled to the US when I was very young for education. It helped me in understanding the entrepreneurial culture there. Before leaving the US, I became a resident; I had the option to settle there, but I decided to come back to India, because I could make a better contribution here than in the US. India at that point was quite backward and poverty levels were very high. I wanted to do something here—that was my line of thinking.

What were the challenges you faced in building the company?
Establishing systems and processes was a technical part of the challenge.

We became a public limited company. I found that it is difficult to establish a sustainable business in India; competing with other companies would be very difficult. I decided that it's very important that if we have to survive as an organization we must look towards the regulatory markets of the US and Europe

We focused on building systems and procedures to compete in the regulatory space. We were one of the early companies to get into the regulatory space.

Have there been missteps along the way?
We were in the top 10 in terms of regulatory filings at one point of time. We could not take advantage of it. In terms of quality systems and understanding the regulatory markets we are second to none. Definitely we made mistakes and it is part of learning. Nobody is perfect. Overall, I am glad (with) where we are today. I think we have a strong foundation, very strong management team. Both the children have joined the business and have a keen interest in it. We have a strong board... I have no regret that we couldn't become a billion-dollar company, but yes, over a period of time we are looking to become a billion-dollar company.

What motivated you to become a better business person?

I wanted to establish a company that will be a quality manufacturer of pharmaceuticals in this country. This is something I felt we can't compromise (on). In spite of difficulties, in terms of certain values and ethics we don't want (to) comprise. That's what has taken the company to this kind of growth and success and a fairly decent name in the industry.

Who are your role models?

J.R.D. Tata, Mahatma Gandhi, Abraham Lincoln. I think these are the people who have done tremendous service to their people without compromising on values. If you look at our board, we have highly successful and extremely good human beings as directors of our company. If you want to build a good organization, you need to keep in touch with good and successful people.

How do you see the future of Neuland Laboratories?

We started as an API company—that is where the core strength of business lies. Going forward, we want to become an end-to-end service provider for the pharmaceutical industry. I think there is huge potential.

15

NextWealth Entrepreneurs Pvt. Ltd

Sridhar Mitta

NEXTWEALTH ENTREPRENEURS PVT. LTD

Founder: Sridhar Mitta

Year of founding: 2009–10

Headquarters: Bangalore

Website: www.nextwealth.in

Area of business: Outsourcing services

Revenue: About $2 million (projected) in 2011–12

Profit: Not disclosed

Uniqueness

*Has a socially oriented goal, facilitating entrepreneurs
to set up business process outsourcing (BPO) delivery
centres in non-urban areas so that talent pool in the
hinterland can be tapped.*

By Sridhar K. Chari

For information technology (IT) industry veteran Sridhar Mitta,
things have come full circle in his post-retirement days—he finds
himself pitching the technical and English language skills of his
delivery teams to sceptical clients. Except that this time around
the clients are not the chief information officers of American
corporations, but Indians in Bangalore, working for both
multinational and Indian companies; and the delivery teams whose
virtues are being peddled are not techies in Bangalore, but techies in
small towns such as Mallasamudram near Salem in Tamil Nadu, and
Chittoor in Andhra Pradesh.

'In some ways, it was easier to convince the Americans,' says Mitta.
'Our own people are wondering, can these people from small towns
do the job?'

Mitta is the managing director of NextWealth Entrepreneurs Pvt.
Ltd, a unique venture aimed at creating IT and business process outsourcing (BPO) delivery centres in small-town India, tapping into a
huge talent pool that might otherwise never enter the IT workforce.

'Past the age of 60, I thought I should retire and use my network and experience. I didn't want to do that with just charity, but actually generate social value. I wanted to harness the talent in small towns in India,' he says.

About 60 per cent of the engineering graduates coming out of the numerous colleges in the country are from small towns, and a sizable percentage of them are girls, according to Mitta. 'Maybe half the boys migrate to cities and with girls, it is less than 5 per cent,' he says.

'So there is a lot of qualified talent that the country has already invested in, which because of family and gender reasons is not utilized. But look at the IT industry. There is high attrition and wages are going up. That is unstable. No wonder jobs are moving to other low-cost countries such as (the) Philippines.'

'If we create this supply from small towns, we can bridge that gap. So the idea is simple: Take engineering talent in small towns, employ them close to home, but deliver the same quality of services. It is a distributed delivery model. If the Indian IT industry in towns is like the mainframe computer, our model is like desktops and laptops. We facilitate entrepreneurs to set up these centres in small towns, give them a majority stake, and provide front-end marketing and other kinds of support,' he says.

Mitta himself hails from a small town—Chittoor.

'Our family had a pharmaceutical business. I was well versed in the business aspects from my childhood, and like my brothers I could have just "joined the shop". But I used to read a magazine called *Electronics Age* published by the Radio Corporation of America. It had a tagline–"Better things for a better world through electronics". Even though I did not quite know what electronics was, I wanted to become an electronics engineer.'

That aspiration took him to a local engineering college. There, he found himself studying tube circuits while transistors had already arrived. So he went to the Indian Institute of Technology, Kharagpur. And that's when he found that the computer revolution was on, and he chased it with a PhD in Oklahoma State University.

He came back to India in 1973 and joined Electronics Corporation of India, which designed computers for defence and space applications.

'Each computer was put together, handmade. It, of course, had less processing power than your phone today, but would cost ₹20-30 lakh. I worked there for seven years. I was following the advent of the 16-bit microprocessor technology, and I felt ECL was not taking a serious enough view of developments. So I joined what was then called Western India Vegetable Products Ltd, and is today Wipro. I became the first employee of Wipro Infotech in 1980.'

At Wipro, they made computers based on Intel processors, which were well received. But change was around the corner with the liberalization in the early 1990s. 'We felt Indian companies might be forced to become just channels. But as R&D (research and development) head, I felt that if the door was open for someone to come in, it was also open for us to go out,' he says.

The perception in the US was that Indians were good in software, and choosing the UNIX platform, they were among the first to provide product development services.

'As we grew, I found that while we used to develop intellectual property, it was work for hire, and so the IP belonged to others. So we wanted to do something for ourselves, and carve a place in Silicon Valley in the US. We decided to set up Nthink in the semiconductor IP business, around 1998.'

Wipro invested in that, and the company also got money from venture capital (VC) funds.

'It gave us an opportunity to look around, and it basically put the entrepreneurial spirit and focus into me. I remember attending a conference at Stanford where the conclusion was that Silicon Valley was what it was because of its ecosystem, and that cannot be recreated elsewhere. So I thought, why can we not create a platform for entrepreneurs to succeed? That became e4e—entrepreneurs for entrepreneurs—co-founded with K.B. Chandrashekar, in 2000. It was different in two ways: We acted like a VC ourselves, but went beyond just giving funds. And the second was that we were offering technology as a service much ahead of time. After seven years, many of the companies were folded back into e4e, and some were sold off.'

Back again in India, with the entrepreneurial urge as strong as ever, Mitta launched NextWealth.

The company gives partnering entrepreneurs a majority stake in the venture. It now has six to eight clients, and is in the process of closing deals with two large American companies, a retailer and an engineering firm, for non-voice BPO work. This ranges from bill processing, human resources, and content management to online mathematics tutoring.

Apart from Chittoor, Mallasamudram, and Amargol near Hubli-Dharwad in Karnataka—NextWealth hopes to start new centres in Madanapalli, Gudiyatham, Erode, and Vijayawada. Mitta hopes NextWealth will have generated 10,000 jobs in a few years, and the model will travel successfully to other companies and towns, besides other developing countries.

For someone who was in at the beginning of the evolution of the Indian IT industry, it continues to be a satisfying journey.

Q&A
SRIDHAR MITTA

How do you hope to create social value with your current venture, Nextwealth?

I saw a great opportunity in the fact there is a lot of unutilized talent in small towns in India. We have a few thousand engineering colleges in this country. A large chunk of them are in small towns, and a sizable percentage of students are girls. Maybe half the boys migrate to cities and with girls, it is less than 5 per cent. So there is a lot of qualified talent that the country has already invested in, which because of family and gender reasons is not utilized.

On the other hand, currently, the IT industry is suffering from a disequilibrium between demand and supply of talent, leading to wage increases and high attrition. So it is becoming less competitive. If we create this supply from small towns, we can bridge that. We facilitate entrepreneurs to set up these centres in small towns, give them a majority stake, and provide front-end marketing and other kinds of support. These entrepreneurs could actually hail from these towns, in some cases.

What does it take for entrepreneurial success in this model?

The person should obviously be capable, but importantly, he or she should be willing to do work with a social bent of mind. Typically, people think they should be retired to do socially relevant projects. But today we are proving that there are opportunities even before retirement.

How do you see the entrepreneurial ecosystem today?

The Indian ecosystem for entrepreneurs is substantially superior to even five years ago. We can no longer make excuses that the ecosystem is not there, in terms of venture funding, angel investors, mentorship, government support, etc. We may not be on a par with Silicon Valley, but most of the things required are there, and they are also being used. So I see a huge growth in the next two years. And the ecosystem will expand too.

What next for Nextwealth and Mitta?

I am in my last innings. My target is getting 10,000 graduates employed in small towns in the next three to four years, from the few hundreds we have now. We want several others to follow this model, other companies in other small towns in India. And then on to other developing countries. We are talking to the Rockefeller Foundation, which is doing a pilot study.

16
Opto Circuits (India) Ltd

At the right place
Vinod Ramnani

OPTO CIRCUITS (INDIA) LTD

Founders: Vinod Ramnani, Thomas Dietiker,
Jayesh Patel, and Usha Ramnani

Year of founding: 1992

Headquarters: Bangalore

Website: www.optoindia.com

Area of business: Medical technology manufacturing

Revenue: $305 million in 2010–11

Profit: $70 million after tax in 2010–11

Uniqueness

*Opto Circuits sells more than 100 products in 150
countries, and aims to become a $1 billion company
by revenue in the next three to four years. It also has
a significant IP portfolio with 168 patents and 53
applications pending with the patent office.*

By Shamsheer Yousaf

Across the road from Bangalore's much-vaunted Infosys Ltd campus
is the headquarters of Opto Circuits (India) Ltd. From the outside,
it looks no different from any of the corporate headquarters in the
neighbourhood. But these buildings house some of the most advanced laboratories in India for one of the country's biggest medical
equipment manufacturers. With $305 million in revenue and $70
million in profit after tax in 2010–11, Opto Circuits has established
itself as a medical equipment firm of some significance. The company sells more than 100 products in about 150 countries, and ended
2010–11 with 41 per cent growth in earnings per share. Revenue,
including those from acquired companies, climbed 47 per cent.

On the other hand, these figures are only a drop in the global medical equipment market, estimated at around $290 billion in 2010,
according to Acmite Market Intelligence.

Chairman and managing director Vinod Ramnani's focus now is on becoming a billion-dollar company in three to four years.

'The total market that we are addressing is huge,' he says. The size of the markets the firm operates in—the invasive and non-invasive segments—is nearly $20 billion in size, according to the company's 2010-11 annual report. 'So even if we have some percentage of it, we will reach $1 billion in 3-4 years.'

The markets in which Opto Circuits operates are growing. The global market for patient-monitoring systems, for example, is estimated to exceed $8 billion by 2015 from around $7 billion in 2008, according to the *Global Markets Direct Report*, 2009.

A mechanical engineer by training, Ramnani's entry into the medical equipment manufacturing industry was a matter of being in the right place at the right time.

'I went to the US (in 1982) two years after I graduated and ended up working in a company that was working on semiconductors,' he says. The semiconductor industry was just picking up steam in the US, and Ramnani learnt a lot about the fledgling industry. Apart from computers, semiconductors began to be used in other applications, including healthcare. 'I got some experience in the healthcare sector and then decided to venture on my own.'

In 1992, Ramnani, along with wife Usha and former colleagues—Thomas Dietiker and Jayesh Patel, decided to set up a manufacturing plant in Bangalore to take advantage of the low cost of labour. 'I was in Bangalore before I went to the US. I knew the place and weather-wise Bangalore was very good for the semiconductor industry. So we got ourselves registered.'

Today, Opto Circuits is a multinational company owning well-known brands such as Cardiac Science, Criticare, Eurocor, Ormed, Mediaid, and Unetixs. Its product profile includes cardiac and vital signs monitoring systems, anesthesia and respiratory care equipment, automated external defibrillators, stents, angioplasty balloons, catheters, and body implants. The company's key markets are North America, Europe, and the BRIC (Brazil, Russia, India, and China) countries.

While Opto Circuits initially made medical equipment for other companies that would then sell the products under their own names, over the past decade it has concentrated on developing and marketing its own products. 'You can't rely entirely on the OEM (original equipment manufacturing) business, which we used to do earlier,' says Ramnani. 'It's a challenging prospect to start from ground zero—we had to develop the product, get all the approvals, including from the US Food and Drug Administration, do market testing, and reliability testing.'

That decision was complemented by an aggressive acquisition strategy; over the past decade, Opto Circuits has purchased 11 companies globally. It bought companies such as Cardiac Sciences to add products such as defibrillators to get ahead of the game. 'Some of the companies which we have bought are our customers,' says Ramnani.

There were other advantages in playing the acquisition game. 'For example, the last company that we bought (Cardiac Sciences), we were also able to sell our other products with their distributors, which would have taken a lot of time to set up.'

The acquisitions also helped the firm build its intellectual property (IP) portfolio. The emphasis Opto Circuits lays on IP can be garnered from the fact that visitors are greeted with a wall of its patents. Since inception, Opto Circuits has acquired 168 patents; another 53 applications are pending with the patent office. 'Growing fast with IP is very important. If a company is available at a good price and has good IP, good synergies, and a good distribution network, I would definitely see it as one of the ways in which you can put yourself on the fast track,' says Ramnani.

As Opto Circuits operates primarily in niche markets, and its products are marketed outside India, most of its competition comes from global firms—including Fortune 500 companies Boston Scientific Corp. and Johnson and Johnson.

To be able to compete with firms of such scale, Opto Circuts has research and development centres in Bangalore, Germany, and the US. Its focus lately has been on making medical technologies more accessible, portable, convergent, connected, and user-friendly by tapping advancements in telemetry, wireless and Bluetooth technology, and networking.

With the $1 billion target firmly in mind, Opto Circuits is looking to consolidate its acquisitions and grow organically for the next few years. 'The good thing is that we have acquired companies that have tremendous growth potential, and we are confident that we will hit that target confidently,' says Ramnani.

Q&A
VINOD RAMNANI

How did the idea of setting up your own firm come about?

When I was in the United States, the first thing that struck me was that there was no job security. There is a lot of uncertainty, and people could be hired or fired anytime... It was completely new to me, and there was a lot of scope for growth which attracted me. People would tell me to explore setting up my own firm, and so I decided to take the plunge.

How was the ecosystem for starting a firm in India back in 1992?

When we started off, we were looking for a suitable place to set up a low-cost manufacturing unit. We explored some places like Indonesia and China, but we finally decided to set up in Bangalore for a few reasons. One, the Indian government was giving some benefits for starting firms at that point of time. Secondly, language wasn't a problem since I was in Bangalore before I went to the US and I knew the place quite well. And thirdly, I thought Bangalore was suited very well as far as weather was concerned, considering this was a semiconductor company.

What were some of the initial challenges and how did you over-come them?

Everything from getting a telephone line to getting a power connection or getting the leaseholder approval was a challenge. Since ours is a 100 per cent export firm, the logistics of getting the material in and out was extremely challenging. To ensure quality, we needed a controlled environment where there is minimum dust in the atmosphere. Setting up these things was a huge challenge. We had no option but to do it. But over time, things started getting better.

What advice do you have for entrepreneurs today?

There are a lot of things out there which are not under your control, things which turn out to be destructive. But you should never say die. Keep your focus right, and just try to make the right decision. You will make mistakes, but as long as you don't repeat them, things will be all right.

17

Pure Chemicals Co.

Business chemistry
N. Ponnuswami

PURE CHEMICALS CO.

Founder: N. Ponnuswami

Year of founding: 1981

Headquarters: Chennai

Website: www.pure-chemical.com

Area of business: Chemical trading

Revenue: ₹1,700 crore in 2010–11

Profit: Not disclosed

Uniqueness

Started a chemical trading business after studying chemistry in high school and expanded the business into a large, internationally recognized company.

By Anupama Chandrasekaran

As the youngest of five children in a family dependent on agriculture, N. Ponnuswami achieved far more than he could have dreamt of.

His company Pure Chemicals Co. is one of the largest chemical distributors in the country, with an eye on becoming one of the global top five.

'Like my brother once said to emphasize the importance of customer service—we should be willing to bring the customer even tiger's milk if he asks for it,' Ponnuswami said in Tamil to illustrate that companies should be ready to do what it takes to serve their customers.

Ponnuswami grew up in Namakkal in central Tamil Nadu as one of four brothers. The family was close to pulling him out of class XII when their father died. But not expecting much economic benefit from dragging Ponnuswami into growing brinjals, groundnuts and rice, the family mutually agreed to send him to college.

After completing his undergraduate degree, Ponnuswami, like most educated youth those days, traveled to Chennai to find work. He lived with a cousin and found a job in a cosmetic factory that made bindis. Soon, for a salary of ₹150 a month, he was put in charge of the small set of women working in the factory.

But Ponnuswami found himself incapable of handling manpower issues and quit the post. He soon found another job, from which he again resigned because of differences with his employer. Chennai seemed too rough for the soft-spoken Ponnuswami.

Angry and dejected with the poor job prospects and pining to be back home, Ponnuswami packed his bags and headed to Namakkal. But his mother and brothers berated him for being meek and defeatist, forcing Ponnuswami to head right back to Chennai. This time he resolved to find a job and stay put.

He asked his cousin to take him under his wing and began working for the chemical trading business for a salary of ₹300. His lodgings were in sparse rooms that housed young bachelors. (One of them was a former bus conductor originally known as Shivaji Rao Gaikwad and studying at the Madras Film Institute. He would later become famous as movie superstar Rajnikanth. Ponnuswami says he would occasionally play chess with the reticent student.)

Ponnuswami worked without a break, opening his cousin's business at 8.30 a.m. every day. Even Sunday was a working day.

'I networked with all the customers and at the bidding of my cousin delivered all goods at no extra charge to the buyers,' said Ponnuswami.

Soon, his family arranged his marriage and the issue of salary came up. His brothers and mother were now hoping Ponnuswami would find a job that could help him manage a family and not just make ends meet. That is when Ponnuswami earnestly thought of starting a business.

He told his cousin and mentor that he wanted to quit and start something on his own in the industrial chemical field that wouldn't compete with his laboratory chemicals business. His cousin showed no ill will and allowed him to go his way.

Discussions began with a numerologist about an appropriate name for the business and in March 1981, with a capital of ₹36,000 and three employees, Ponnuswami launched Pure Chemicals Co. He set a target of ₹1 lakh in monthly revenue for the first year but logged just ₹21,000 the first month.

Business picked up over the next few months and he did end up with ₹12 lakh in revenue the first year, which brought in a profit of ₹1 lakh.

He started adding more customers and politely asked that they make payments within a week instead of the standard practice of a month, so that he could buy more stock and service them well. In the second year itself, sales doubled to ₹25 lakh.

Ponnuswami recalls he would pay customers to return the empty chemical cans that his team would clean up and reuse. Within Chennai, Ponnuswami would get his employees to deliver stock in a cycle cart. But when orders started pouring in from other parts of Tamil Nadu, it was hard to find truck owners willing to carry acids and other chemicals along with other stock in their vehicles.

Ponnuswami braved the odds and set up branches in other parts of Tamil Nadu to service his clients.

'Immediately, we were competitive as transportation costs were reduced and we were able to eliminate all our competitors,' Ponnuswami said.

It was 1990, and the company's turnover was touching ₹5 crore. It was around this time that the Pure Chemicals founder started hiring management and engineering graduates to expand his company. Branches were set up in other parts of India.

However, Ponnuswami was late in entering the business of importing and selling chemicals. Pure Chemicals started importing products only in 2000—a decade after India's economy opened up and the government reduced duties on chemical imports. His competitors had moved at a faster pace.

'We would have been a ₹5,000 crore company if I had moved quickly on the chemical importing business but I was conservative,' Ponnuswami admits.

Today, the company's revenue stands at ₹1,700 crore. Ponnuswami expects this to grow at least 45 per cent in 2012.

And, the entrepreneur is fervently trying not to repeat past mistakes or miss opportunities. This time around, he isn't afraid to think big.

Ponnuswami's eyes are set on overseas growth with the target to be within the top five globally. The company has branches in Sri Lanka, Singapore, Bangladesh, and Kenya. It also has a small procurement office in China.

'The US and Europe are mature markets and so we are focusing our energies on the Middle East, Africa, and the Asia-Pacific region,' Ponnuswami said.

Q&A
N. PONNUSWAMI

What would you attribute your success to?
Customer service–the lesson I learnt from my cousin who was running a chemical laboratory, where I started working: do what the customer asks. It is vital to meet the urgent need of a customer. It is okay to spend a little money and effort to deliver chemicals on time to customers. It will reflect in the business later as they will not forget the service provided.

What are the turning points in your journey as an entrepreneur?
I started the business by borrowing money from my family and relatives. The first order gave me real confidence to begin. It was one drum of acetone supplied to Amrutanjan and I made a profit of ₹3,000. We had difficulty transporting huge acid barrels to other towns in Tamil Nadu. Setting up the first depot in Erode helped deliver chemicals to customers sooner and cut down on transportation costs. In the mid-90s, changing the recruitment policy to hire employees with domain knowledge such as chemical engineers and (people with) a master's degree in chemistry (was also a turning point). My employees have better expertise selling chemicals than my competitors.

Looking back, is there anything you would have done differently?
We should have started imports soon after liberalization. Back then, I had limited knowledge and was focused on appointing employees. I was conservative in my approach. Only when we lost some good agencies did I realize that the company must start imports. We started only in 2000, almost a decade later. Earlier, I used to feel that I was not an industrialist manufacturing products but later realized that I should give my best effort in the business I was pursuing.

What are your growth plans?
We are currently a leading chemical distribution company in India with a turnover of ₹1,700 crore. In global ranking, we would be somewhere around the 32nd position and our ambition is to reach the fifth position. We plan to focus on

the Asia-Pacific region, West Asia, and Africa. Pure Chemicals has offices in Sri Lanka, Dubai, Melbourne, and Kenya (and) will set up operations in Singapore and Bangladesh shortly.

What qualities should an entrepreneur possess to be successful?
First, select a business that is scalable. Secondly, don't be egoistic. And finally, delegate work with responsibility and try not to micromanage.

18

Ramraj Cotton

Dhoti fashion
K.R. Nagaraj

RAMRAJ COTTON

Founder: K.R. Nagaraj

Year of founding: 1983

Headquarters: Tirupur

Website: ramrajcotton.in

Area of business: Textiles: dhotis, shirts, and innerwear

Revenue: Not disclosed

Profit: Not disclosed

Uniqueness

At a time when the traditional south Indian cloth was threatened, K.R. Nagaraj brought the dhoti back into vogue. Adding white belts and cellphone pouches to the product portfolio helped address issues youngsters faced while trying on the garment.

By Amritha Venketakrishnan

K.R. Nagaraj is not just a fast talker, he also acts fast.

Over almost two decades, the high-school graduate, who passed his class XII examination at the second attempt, has inched closer to the ₹1,000 crore revenue mark for his company, which makes varieties of the traditional white dhoti.

In the era of trousers, Nagaraj, 52, has brought the dhoti—worn mostly by south Indian men—back into vogue; he has even added value to the garment by introducing belts and mobile phone pouches.

Nagaraj was born 14 km outside of Tirupur, Tamil Nadu's textile hub that's also called dollar city because of its export focus, which earns it valuable foreign exchange. His farming family wanted him to try for a government job.

'In the village, we used to look up to our teachers and back then I thought becoming a teacher would be a good idea as the ₹1,000 pay was attractive,' Nagaraj says. 'But then there would also be frequent visitors who arrived in spotless white attire in an Ambassador car. Inevitably, they were always part of Tirupur's textile industry despite having completed just primary level schooling. I realized to be able to buy a car or be successful you did not need a degree.'

When he was 16 years old, his father asked Nagaraj to hop on to his bicycle for a ride. Halfway through, the teenager learnt that his father had got him a bill-collector's job at the local government office.

When he found out where they were going, he jumped off the cycle, telling his father he would rather be a tea boy than work as a bill collector. That very day he came across a small textile store and asked the owner for a job, joining that evening for a salary of ₹60 a month.

Nagaraj took on various sales and marketing jobs in the local garments business and even travelled to neighbouring Andhra Pradesh as a sales representative despite not knowing Telugu, the language of the state.

'Initially, it was difficult but I learnt to read sign boards, cinema posters, etc., and now I'm more comfortable in Telugu than Tamil,' he says. 'This is where I learnt what marketing really was and how difficult it is to sell.'

Following a failed venture with friends, Nagaraj contemplated launching his own dhoti business. To begin with, he wanted to do away with the commonly used khadi label since the product was machine-woven cotton. And secondly, he worked at making the dhoti thicker than its flimsier avatar which made it less wearable.

In 1983, the Ramraj brand was born.

'The only difference between a ₹2 coffee in a small hotel and a ₹50 coffee at a five-star hotel is the presentation,' says Ramraj. 'So I too wanted to present my product differently and people accepted it. I set out to change the way people viewed dhotis and succeeded.'

Nagaraj was relentless in his pursuit to make the antiquated garment relevant. He wanted to do something about the handmade knot that's expected to hold up a dhoti, and always presents the danger of a wardrobe malfunction.

'Back then there were only black belts in the market, which looked bad when clubbed with a white dhoti. So I brought in the white belt, and now the sale of that is equal to that of a dhoti,' Nagaraj says.

Nagaraj himself abandoned trousers to wear dhotis all the time, much to the embarrassment of his wife, who saw her husband being turned away at posh hotels because of his attire.

'I started wearing the dhoti at the age of 25 and have not looked back since,' Nagaraj says.

The Ramraj dhotis at ₹100 a piece were four times the price of regular ones. Nagaraj had to assure shopkeepers he would take back the merchandise if it didn't sell. Despite such promises, he found it tough to convince shopkeepers in the 1980s to stock more than 5-10 pieces.

So in 1993, Nagaraj focused his energies on marketing the dhoti and improving its image. He came up with an advertisement campaign that showed men wearing Ramraj dhotis being allowed into top hotels and given due respect. Ten years after its launch, the brand started gaining a foothold in the market.

'Had I known initially what an uphill battle running this was going to be, I may not have gone into this business,' Nagaraj says.

By 2004, the Ramraj brand was the established market leader in the southern states, with the company claiming 80 per cent of the market. 'After a certain time you get saturated and stop, invest in real estate or some form of security. But I put everything back into the business because I had the confidence that it would bear fruit,' Nagaraj says.

The company is now looking beyond south India to enter Maharashtra and Gujarat next year, and then West Bengal and Orissa. Overseas, Dubai is a lucrative market, Nagaraj says.

When the government announced in August 2010 that it was open to bids for airport shops, Nagaraj jumped at the opportunity. Airport stores, he says, are a great vehicle to market and advertise the brand.

'My dream is to take this worldwide and this is the first step. It is more for people to recognize the brand and this is the right platform for it. In fact, there was a US citizen who came to our shop (at Chennai airport) and bought four dhotis after I explained to him that it was part of our culture and how important it was to us,' he says.

Funding for the ventures could come through a stock market listing and the next generation—his daughter and son-in-law—are working towards that, says the creator of the Ramraj brand.

There are challenges—rising labour costs, finding tailors and weavers. But he refuses to lose sleep over such problems. 'I look at myself as a salaried manager of the business and not as an owner,' he says.

Q&A
K.R. NAGARAJ

What were the hurdles you faced along the way?

There was a time when producers tried to market their goods directly (and) they were able to sell at a much cheaper price. So this meant I had to move out of certain markets. Some of these producers lacked marketing prowess and came back to me, but this situation got me thinking about production in 1987–88 and I was able to take this forward because people were ready to give me raw material on credit.

Tell us about how you handled a specific challenge?

I entered Andhra Pradesh first because it was a known market to me. But when I brought in the four-metre dhoti to Tamil Nadu I did not find any takers because the two-metre dhoti was more popular here. So I was stuck with a big stock of four-metre dhotis with no way out. Then I asked the sales team to market the dhotis to the upper middle class and high-end customers by selling it as a product that would set them apart from others wearing the traditional two-meter dhotis, and soon sales picked up and this became a trend.

Going forward, what can we expect from you?

Our plan is to take this to a pan-India level in the next five years and then worldwide. I've started a new brand for ladies called Ramyam, which is a shirt top. I have not ventured into exports directly till now, as there have been sales only through dealers. Dubai has a lot of demand for this material, so we will look into that next.

We are looking to get the business ready for an IPO (initial public offer) sometime in the future. My son-in-law and daughter have both started to steer the company in that direction.

What is an important lesson you would ask entrepreneurs to keep in mind?

Delegation is key. From just one, I now have 205 marketing professionals. I have over 19,000 families depending on my company.

The Chennai outlet rode on the success of what had become the chain's flagship sweet—the melt-in-your-mouth Mysurpa, a softer version of the Mysorepak made of chickpea flour, ghee, and sugar.

The Mysorepak, a household South Indian sweet, is much loved for its buttery firm sweetness and yet much feared for the dental tenacity required to bite into its tough innards.

It would have been nothing short of sacrilege to tweak the age-old recipe of this revered rocky treat. But the late Iyer did just that.

He tinkered with the procedure to concoct a softer, delicate version of the calorific sweet, which flew off his restaurant's shelves as customers indulged in the fudge-like avatar.

His sons imbibed the same love for the product.

'One cannot separate Mysurpa and me,' says Murali, partly revealing his family's philosophy towards the business and the intuitiveness that comes from understanding customers and sweets. 'I am part of the product.'

Murali's sweet adventure started at the age of 16 in his father's 200 sq. ft. Sri Krishna Bhavan restaurant in Coimbatore, a city in the foothills of the Western Ghats. The sweet stall was just a small cog in the restaurant machine.

He donned many hats—that of a dosa master, cleaner, cashier, and even waiter—at the family-owned eatery. That is where his love for food started.

The most important lesson he learnt from his father was to break existing conventions in a market known for its stubborn food habits.

'He changed the way people viewed sweets,' Murali said in Tamil of his father.

'He was bold enough to announce that his sweets were in fact made of pure ghee,' whereas in those days sweet shops would put out signs in big bold letters reading 'Pure Ghee Sweets' and would in small font add 'not' within brackets, he recalls.

That's perhaps similar to deals today advertised with an asterisk indicating that conditions apply.

'He could tell just by looking at something based on colour and smell if it had salt or not,' says Murali, who holds the same high quality standards his father set by ensuring that his sweets are made from pure ghee.

SPREADING WINGS

While the brothers were comfortable growing the business in Coimbatore, the second largest city in Tamil Nadu, Murali was itching to make a dent in the state's capital—Chennai.

After starting the first store in the city fifteen years ago, Murali has expanded the chain to 26 outlets, a number he plans to increase to 100 within two years, and to take it to the US and the UK, where Indians crave for that little slice of home.

To be sure, it hasn't all been an easy ride for the 63-year-old business. Murali admits that his passion to return to his family's roots through Rassa, a fine dining restaurant venture, is yet to taste success.

True to its heritage, the restaurant tries to serve time-tested recipes with a twist. Vethalai (betel leaf) biriyani is one such item on the menu and coconut water payasam, or rice pudding, is another.

'People think we are only about sweets. We need to prove we can excel here as well and establish a different identity,' says the 51-year-old mathematics graduate.

Gokulam, which serves up Indian fast food like dahi vada, masala dosa, and chaat items such as bhelpuri, is another venue he hopes to expand.

In Chennai, Sri Krishna has under its banner over 250 varieties of sweets and savouries, which come from a state-of-the-art 50,000 sq. ft kitchen that is an hour's drive from the city. The facility cost nearly ₹6 crore to set up.

Upgrading from a modest eight-stove kitchen to 150 burners in the sweet factory is necessary not just for expansion and standardized quality, but also to gear up for demand spikes in the festive season, such as during Diwali.

Planning and preparation for such events start a month before the festival day as sales quadruple, says Murali.

He keeps an eagle eye on the market to spot a business opportunity. When he discovered that working women were hard pressed for time to cook specific sweets and savouries for smaller family festivals, he innovated special packages that included even the puja items like a lamp or an idol used for worship. He also drew inspiration from chocolate truffle packages and introduced 36 bite-sized sweet items, a bit like petit fours, packed in a convenient gift box.

'Previously people bought sweets for a purpose, for instance when guests were expected. Now when you visit someone even informally, you take with you a box of SKS,' he says of the rationale for the gift box, which bear the initials of the chain's name.

COMPETITION ON THE HEELS

Murali estimates that today a customer can afford to spend on average around ₹300-500 on sweets a month. But even as customer spending increases, competition is keeping pace.

Thirty-year-old south Chennai-based rival The Grand Sweets and Snacks, which had just one branch all these years, is expanding rapidly and has opened six new branches in a year.

While competition doesn't unnerve Murali, he does feel the pressure of losing customers in the face of the rising cost of raw materials such as oil and milk.

'We cannot raise the selling price after a certain limit because of competition,' he says.

Rocketing real estate prices have now got him thinking about less expensive models such as smaller express counters in malls and information technology parks.

To Murali, the customer is like family.

'It is not an agreement or transaction between the customer and SKS. My product has a life. How happy the customers are with my products determines my success,' he said. 'Even today I am not perfect. Every day I try to be a little bit closer to my product.'

Q&A
M. MURALI

Take us back to the start of your journey in Chennai. What was that like?

When I first came to Chennai I had no plans of staying as my family was back in Coimbatore. But the kind of response I received after I opened my first store in 1996 in T. Nagar was phenomenal. The love of the Chennai people has kept me rooted here. The potential here is enormous, we can even set up 100 stores here.

What are the lessons you have learnt from your father?

My father led by example and never advised me. In the beginning, the growth in the business was value-based growth. We constantly looked at improving our products. My father was a very good administrator. He knew how to get the work done from the employees. He was dedicated. You cannot separate me from SKS Mysurpa. I am part of the product. My father was the same way.

How do you see the growth of Sri Krishna?

There was no concept of exclusive sweet shops earlier and it came about only in the 1970s and we opened up stores in Coimbatore. I had around 7-8 burners in Chennai in my stores and now have 150-200 burners in the Nemam facility, where I have a 50,000 sq. ft kitchen. This not only helps expansion but also to maintain a standardized taste and quality (across the 26 stores) in the city.

What are the challenges you face?

Prices of raw materials are increasing every day and we cannot raise the selling price after a certain limit because of competition. So this is a constant challenge we face. Rassa, a fine-dining restaurant venture, has also not taken off as we had hoped. We need to show people we can excel at this as well.

What is the one thing you would stress with regard to your products?

My brother (M. Krishnan), like my father, is very serious about quality. If it is not good we throw it out. At any given point in time, we never compromise on this. Making first time customers come back to the store and growing that loyalty is important as they will become ambassadors for our products.

— ◈ —

20

Stovekraft Pvt. Ltd

Cooking a growth story
Rajendra J. Gandhi

STOVEKRAFT PVT. LTD

Founder: Rajendra J. Gandhi
Year of founding: 1999
Headquarters: Bangalore
Website: www.stovekraft.com
Area of business: Kitchen appliances
Revenue: ₹900 crore in 2010–11
Profit: Not disclosed

Uniqueness

A strong focus on tying up raw material suppliers to avert any supply-side constraints. Stovekraft has also expanded its presence across all customer segments. To cater to price-conscious customers who put value above all, Yogendra Gandhi launched two brands in 2002. At the other end of the market, he signed a deal with an Italian modular kitchen company in 2009 to sell premium kitchens in India.

By Byravee Iyer

Rajendra Gandhi is candid that he benefited from his Marwadi business roots. In the 1990s, Gandhi worked as a salesman in Vardhaman, the family business that sold kitchen appliances in Bangalore's residential hub Jayanagar. His sights though were set on doing something much bigger.

In 1999, Gandhi took a calculated risk and started his own venture—Stovekraft Pvt. Ltd, initially a supplier of cookware parts before it turned into a full-fledged manufacturer of kitchen appliances. Soon, he got his first customer, a maker of gas stoves who wanted Gandhi to make the bodies for the items. The customer advanced ₹1.5 lakh and Gandhi invested some of his own savings into Stovekraft. 'And I've never looked back,' says Gandhi. Indeed, Stovekraft broke even in the first year itself, making

₹24 lakh. For the next seven years it grew at an enviable 100 per cent annually.

Stovekraft began supplying the bodies to TTK Prestige, Bharat Petroleum Corp. Ltd, and Hindustan Petroleum Corp. Ltd. Its move from supplier to manufacturer happened by chance when a key customer, a gas stove manufacturer, began going out of business. Stovekraft stepped in and started making gas stoves in 2002 and eventually exited the business of supplying parts to other firms. 'Unfortunately, we couldn't continue the OEM (original equipment manufacturer) business for long. We eventually started our own brands,' says Gandhi.

Stovekraft launched two brands—Pigeon and Gilma—in 2002. Pigeon is a bottom-of-the-pyramid brand selling gas stoves, pressure cookers, and mixer grinders. Gilma is the premium brand, sold through, franchisee-managed stores. Gilma sells gas stoves, water heaters and modular kitchens.

Stovekraft targets two lucrative markets—one derived from large-scale urbanization and the other from the low penetration of pressure cookers and gas stoves in the villages. To boost the spread of liquefied petroleum gas (LPG), currently having a 19 per cent share, in rural India, the government is handing out incentives such as community kitchens in villages to improve its reach. As for pressure cookers, high replacement demand has spurred growth. Moreover, the company also exports kerosene stoves to Sri Lanka, West Asia, and the Fiji Islands.

All this has helped Stovekraft become the market leader in the LPG gas segment with a share of about 25 per cent. It is also the leader in the non-stick cookware segment, and has about a 10 per cent market share in the pressure cooker category, which makes it the third-largest maker of the implements in the country. It is now diversifying into electric chimneys, ovens, and kitchen hobs.

In 2010–2011, the company posted revenue of ₹900 crore, growing at a compounded annual growth rate of 68 per cent. This is well above the market growth rate of about 35 per cent, according to Gandhi. What's helped is that from being a Bangalore-based company, Stovekraft has expanded its reach across Karnataka, Tamil Nadu,

Andhra Pradesh, Kerala, and Goa. And it's gaining ground in Maharashtra, Gujarat, Rajasthan, West Bengal, Jharkhand, and Orissa.

It now has two factories—one each in Bangalore and Himachal Pradesh—and its employee base has risen from five in 1999 to 2,000 in 2011.

All this expansion required external funding. In 2007, Stovekraft raised ₹22 crore through SIDBI Venture Capital and more recently ₹50 crore from Sequoia Capital.

A strong distribution network is key for a business like Stovekraft. To that end it has tied up with Indian Oil Corp., Bharat Petroleum Corp., and Hindustan Petroleum Corp. for the supply of co-branded LPG stoves. Through these partnerships, Stovekraft's products are present across 20,000 outlets in little known pockets in rural India. That apart, it is present in about 40,000 multibrand retail outlets. The premium Gilma brand, however, is only sold through a hundred or so exclusive outlets.

Stovekraft's expansion hasn't been without its share of challenges. Growth in the domestic kitchen appliances market has attracted multinationals. In 2011, Royal Philips Electronics acquired Chennai-based Maya Appliances, owner of the Preethi brand that sells a host of products including gas stoves, electric cookers, and mixer-grinders.

With Philips' strong distribution network, Preethi could shake up things for Stovekraft. 'This industry never had large international players,' says Gandhi. 'Now over the last few years it has begun to attract their attention because of the strong growth rate.'

Gandhi himself is no stranger to acquisitions. In fact, he has used this strategy to ensure smooth supply-side dynamics. Over the years he has purchased stakes in various raw material suppliers including rolling mills and aluminium companies. 'Our supply wasn't matching our growth so we had to ensure that there were no supply-side constraints,' Gandhi points out.

Stovekraft is also keen to tie up with big international firms. In 2009, it signed a joint venture with Spagnol Cucine, an Italian modular kitchen company, to sell premium kitchens in India. Stovekraft is also talking with a couple of non-stick cookware companies for tie-ups.

— ◈ —

Q&A
RAJENDRA GANDHI

What prompted you to start your own business?
It was my experience in the retail business with my father. I thought that while catering to housewives' requirements at the store, why not get into manufacturing these products that would really delight them. Of course, it was not only about selling but also producing these products.

From being a small Bangalore-based company you're slowly expanding your presence in India. How did that expansion happen?
It's about growth. Once you cater to requirements closer to you, you want to move out. First we spread ourselves across south India and now we have a strong presence in all four southern states and Goa. And now we've expanded to Maharashtra, Gujarat, and Rajasthan and in the last two years we've been building our markets in West Bengal, Jharkand, and Orissa.

What is the competitive landscape like in the kitchen solutions business?
Our evolution in this industry was a threat to our competition. We have made the industry more serious about this business. With the industry growing at the rate it is, it is now attracting lot of attention from large players. We had very small players earlier, but going forward large players including multinationals are interested in this space.

What is Stovekraft's revenue model?
We have two brands. The first is Pigeon, which caters to the bottom of the pyramid. Meanwhile, our premium brand Gilma is sold only through company-owned franchisee outlets. We have a distribution dealer chain for our Pigeon brand.

When did you break even?
Stovekraft started in 1999 to cater to the requirements of the OEM businesses. One such original equipment manufacturer had developed a gas stove and they wanted us to manage it. They approached us because they saw val-

ue in doing business with us. We were considered a low-cost manufacturing business. Unfortunately, we couldn't continue the OEM business for long, and eventually started our own brands. By 2000, we came out of the OEM business and there is the evolution of Stovekraft. We've never had a loss from Day 1, except in the year 2008–2009, when we had a fire in the factory and some forex loss as well. Otherwise we've never had a gestation period.

When did the business reach an inflection point?

I think (with) the launch of our aluminum pressure cooker in 2004, we got an unprecedented response. We built a factory with a capacity to produce 25,000 cookers, but orders for that month alone were 25,000 and just from one state. And we had no choice but to expand that very month.

21

Suguna Poultry

B. Soundararajan

SUGUNA POULTRY

Founder: B. Soundararajan

Year of founding: 1986

Headquarters: Coimbatore

Website: www.sugunapoultry.com

Area of business: Poultry farming—eggs, broiler chicken, and processed meat

Pevenue: ₹3,720 crore

Profit: Not disclosed

Uniqueness

Having pioneered the concept of contract farming in the 1980s, B. Soundararajan and his company hope to change the Indian consumer's attitude towards chicken and make it part of the regular diet by introducing special go-to stores to sell processed meat.

By Amritha Venketakrishnan

What came first? The chicken or the egg? B. Soundararajan may just know the answer to this rusty riddle.

The 50-year-old businessman is the founder and owner of Suguna Poultry Farm Ltd, a ₹3,700 crore company that's India's No. 1 and the world's sixth largest broiler producer. It took a quarter of a century to grow from being a contract farmer to its present position, offering the lesson that it takes time for a good idea to hatch.

Soundararajan, who has spent half his life in the poultry business, was born near Udumalpet—a west Tamil Nadu town ensconced in the hills. A young Soundararajan saw his town—known as 'the poor man's Ooty'—and its surrounding areas receive rain showers twice a year, supporting crops such as groundnut, cotton, maize, and sugar cane the year round.

His father advised him to skirt a diploma course that could only lead to a low-paying government job and encouraged him to dig

143

into the family's farmland instead. So in 1978, the then 17-year-old high-school graduate entered the labour-intensive activity of growing vegetables such as brinjal and tomato.

But at the start of the 1980s, the rains petered out, the ground-water receded and labour became expensive. Fluctuating vegetable prices didn't cover costs so the business had to be closed down.

'My father gave me the freedom to make my own decisions,' said Soundararajan. 'He did not restrict me. Even after the initial agriculture venture failed he was not critical.'

Soundararajan soon took up a less challenging job with his brother-in-law who sold farm equipment and did that for four years. He heard about the poultry business in 1983 from an uncle, who was venturing into that space. It was the start of a 25-year-long journey.

He embarked on cattle and poultry farming with ₹5,000 from his mother, who had to hock her jewellery to borrow the money. Shortly afterwards, Soundararajan realized that chicken and eggs offered better returns than cattle and expanded his focus by diversifying into poultry feed. In 1990, the business that was launched with a capital of a few thousand rupees was logging ₹2 crore in revenue.

But before Soundararajan could rejoice, calamity struck. Prices crashed because of an oversupply of chicken and farmers who had borrowed to buy stock from the company went out of business and also defaulted on loans taken from Suguna worth ₹15 lakh.

'I was nearing bankruptcy at this point and had chit fund loans worth ₹6-7 lakh hanging like a knife over my head,' said Soundararajan, whose company used to sell chicks from the hatcheries to the farmer, who then bore the risk of price fluctuations.

'After talking to a lot of farmers, we realized that the business was unviable during times of oversupply of birds.'

The poultry businessman also knew that the farmers did not deliberately renege on the debt and chalked out a plan that was later validated by an article he read in American magazine *Watt Poultry*. The farmer offered land and labour while the company provided chicks, feed, and vaccines. The farmer got a fee for taking care of the chicks that Suguna picked up from the farm gate after six weeks, when they were ready to be sold.

Over the next decade the company touched the ₹7 crore sales mark and seemed poised to expand around the state but again a supply glut hit Suguna, which had come to own the chickens. This time the mild-natured Soundararajan's employees lent him money and bailed him out—a gesture he finds hard to forget during his day-to-day interaction with his workers, most of whom have remained with him over the long term. With this capital he moved to other states, offsetting his losses, and got back on the growth track.

Suguna's farmers collective today stands at 17,000 in 11 states, handling 730,000 tonnes of chicken. In 1990, it had two-three farmers in Tamil Nadu managing 200 birds. As the company expanded, farmers in the various states abandoned middlemen and got a better price as they dealt directly with the broiler producer.

'Governments felt that this model helped rural development and empowered the farmer,' Soundararajan said.

In 2002, the entrepreneur invested in a chicken-processing plant but with 97 per cent of chicken consumption being of the freshly cut variety, unlike the widespread usage of frozen meat abroad, Soundararajan felt the need to set up retail outlets called Suguna Daily Fresh, supplying eight million birds a week.

And a few years later, in 2006, the World Bank's International Finance Corporation picked up a 5 per cent stake in the company for $11 million.

Proving that the poultry business can be a roller-coaster ride, the monetary lift was followed quickly by a slide. Soundararajan's business crashed in 2008 due to the spread of bird flu infections that made people fearful of consuming poultry. Losses touched ₹90-100 crore that year even as input costs such as bird feed skyrocketed. This time—having learned from previous occasions—the company had sufficient cash in reserve to keep its head above the water.

Suguna Poultry is hoping to maintain its annual growth pace at 12-15 per cent and steadily tap into the ₹25,000 crore Indian poultry industry that is expected to touch ₹80,000 crore by 2020.

Soundararajan is hoping that Suguna will be a ₹4,000 crore company this year and is aiming at making management increasingly professional. He himself stepped down from the post of managing director a few months ago.

Other Asian territories with a lower population but higher per capita consumption—four times that of India's 3 kg—offer export potential.

'The conversion of Indian customers towards processed meat is both a challenge, and an opportunity,' Soundararajan said.

Q&A
B. SOUNDARARAJAN

How did the idea of contract farming come about?

In 1990, many farmers we worked with closed down their farms because it was no longer viable as the price variations were very high. The farmers were good producers and had good poultry management systems. But we didn't want to burden them with costs and losses. Instead of giving them credit, we decided to give them inputs and make them produce chickens. The farmers would be entitled to conversion charges or growing charges. Farmers were comfortable with this as it was an assured income without having to take on market risks. So we supply the day-old chicks, feed, medicines, and technical supervision. The farmer had to have the land, shed, water, power, and poultry management... In value terms, around 8 per cent of the total input cost the farmer will get as conversion charges.

So how do you mitigate your risk?

We have 50 veterinary doctors and 1,200 field officers to manage the health of the chicks. We can predict to an extent the good and bad periods in the market given our experience. On a yearly basis we will make profits, but quarter-on-quarter we cannot generate the profits.

What is your outlook for the market?

India's per capita consumption is just a quarter of Sri Lanka and Bangladesh, where it ranges between 10 kg and 12 kg. But that means India will be on a 15-20% annual growth trajectory for the next 20 years. This is a ₹25,000 crore industry and every year ₹4,000 crore of additional consumption happens and out of this, ₹1,000-1,500 crore we can take easily.

Where do you see your company in the coming years?

Expanding to other countries is key and about a year back we started to produce and sell in Sri Lanka and Bangladesh—each contributing ₹10-20 crore of revenue. We are also eying Vietnam and the Philippines. It is better to enter these underdeveloped markets than developed, mature markets in the US and Europe.

147

Are you charting a succession plan?
In terms of ownership, we'd like to keep it family-owned. My son is keen on taking over the reins at some point. Meanwhile, my brother and I are scouting for new opportunities in agriculture and may consider entering the dairy space and seed production.

22

TD Power Systems Ltd

Power shift
Nikhil Kumar

TD POWER SYSTEMS LTD

Founder: Nikhil Kumar

Year of founding: 2001

Headquarters: Bangalore

Website: www.tdps.co.in

Area of business: Generator manufacturing

Revenue: ₹875 crore in 2010–11

Net profit: ₹56 crore in 2010–11

Uniqueness

*A generator manufacturing company out of India trying to
make a name for itself on the global engineering products
stage with the 'made in India' label. What works for it is
a Japanese-like focus on quality, courtesy the company's
origins. The ability to make custom-designed generators help
it compete with BHEL Ltd.*

By P. Manoj

In 1999, Toyo Denki Seizo KK, a manufacturer of power and electrical equipment in Japan, was shutting its generator-making plant.
Toyo Denki supplied large electric generators to India and had a
working relationship with Kirloskar Electric Co. Ltd, where Nikhil
Kumar worked as a general manager. Kumar knew Hitoshi Matsuo,
the general manager of Toyo Denki, and was informed about the im-
minent closure. The due got together and asked Toyo Denki if it was
willing to sell the business to them.

'Toyo Denki said that they would not be able to do much except
give us five sets of designs. And so they gave us five sets of drawings in
a file and said, "Okay, now do whatever you want to do with this",'
recalls Kumar, the joint managing director of TD Power Systems Ltd.
Kumar and Matsuo paid $100,000 to Toyo Denki for parting with
the five drawings.

Back in India, Kumar and Matsuo looked around for someone

to fund them to start a company. Banks were of no help because they had no collateral to offer. Finally, Mumbai-based Shamrao Vithal Co-operative Bank Ltd came to their rescue, offering a loan of ₹4 crore.

Mohib N. Khericha, now the non-executive chairman of TD Power, put in a substantial but undisclosed amount of equity as a financial investor. Kumar and Matsuo pooled in another ₹1 crore. 'It was Shamrao Vithal Co-operative Bank and Mohib who had the faith to put money in us and trusted us to go into business,' says Kumar, sitting in his office located inside the factory Matsuo and he built in 2001 at Nelamangala on the outskirts of Bangalore.

'It was a huge risk I took at that time,' says Kumar, who studied engineering at the regional engineering college in Suratkal, Karnataka. 'I had no choice, I had to do something with my life. I wasn't thinking when this chance came along. This was a line of business I was familiar with, I knew it was a great business to be in. I also knew there were huge challenges.'

TD Power started with manufacturing large electric generators based on drawings bought from the defunct Japanese outfit. The duo finally ended up doing everything themselves—localizing the drawings/designs for generators to suit Indian grid conditions and customer requirements, designing smaller generators of 1-10 MW, and even designing hydroelectric and diesel generators and wind turbines.

Initially, TD Power found it difficult to sell the machines because it was up against a giant—Bharat Heavy Electricals Ltd. 'We were up against a wall,' reminisces Kumar, a former national badminton player. 'BHEL had a stranglehold on this market, people only trusted this one brand.'

However, with a lot of persuasion and attractive pricing, TD Power won over a few private sector customers. It was these customers that gave Kumar and Matsuo the hope that they could make it if they supplied good machines. It took a while and was a long uphill struggle.

'You cannot crack BHEL by supplying one or two machines. You need to have an installed base of some 200 machines. And it was only in the fifth or sixth year of operations that we really started seeing the multiplier effect or universal acceptance of our products all over India,' Kumar says.

TD Power is strong in Southeast Asia, the Asia-Pacific, Japan, India, and West Asia and is trying to penetrate Europe and the US as well. It faces the same challenges in these markets as it did initially in India. Generators encompassing stem, gas, hydro-electric, and wind are a multi-billion dollar industry worldwide, dominated by ABB Ltd, Siemens AG, General Electric Corp., Toshiba Corp., Mitsubishi Corp., and Hitachi Ltd.

'We have speed, flexibility, response, and a good product. Once customers find we make equally good machines and give even better service at a much more competitive price and the shift starts taking place, these MNCs will find it difficult to compete against us,' Kumar says.

Though TD Power has managed to earn a good set of customers in Europe, Kumar says there are 'acceptance issues' in that region for engineering products made in India. 'We are battling the "made in India" tag in Europe. We have to prove ourselves as an exception rather than the rule. It's where the software industry was 20 years ago, like Infosys and Wipro trying to make a breakthrough into Europe and America in the early 1990s to prove that the Indian software industry can really do a good job... It takes time to have a universal acceptance like say "a made in Germany" or "a made in Japan" product.'

TD Power is ramping up its capacity with a new factory, it's second, just 2 km from the existing one, with funds raised from an initial public offering of its shares in August 2011.

The company sold about 26 per cent of its shares to raise ₹227 crore from investors including Capital Research, Sequoia Capital, IDFC Mutual, and Axis Bank at a time the stock markets were roiled by Standard and Poor's downgrade of US treasury debt. The new factory will double TD Power's manufacturing capacity.

Large electric generators involve a great deal of manual intervention. It's a highly skilled job and operators have to be trained extensively.

'Quality is the only thing that sells. You can be one-tenth the price of Toshiba, but if you don't have the quality no one's going to buy your machines,' Kumar says. 'These electric generators would power an entire industrial complex. If the machine breaks down or shuts down for even two minutes, the entire process industry will shut down. It's a machine critical application.'

Q&A
NIKHIL KUMAR

What do you think is a key element for success as an entrepreneur?
Having a good core team of people and working with them effectively because one person cannot do everything. Work hard, shun ego to a large extent to be able to take humiliation in your stride and be able to go through the downs, and hold your head up high and have the perseverance to come up.

The third thing—not in the hands of the entrepreneur—is to have a little bit of luck. I can't define it, you can have everything but if you don't have luck you are not going to make it.

Is funding an issue today for budding entrepreneurs in India?
Funding is less of an issue today. Entrepreneurs have multiple avenues—private equity, venture capital, etc.—which was not there 12 years ago; maybe it was there but not so pervasive as it is today. Investors are also no fools. Even when money is available, you need to have a strong business plan, strong product to get funding. Maybe it is more difficult to raise money today than it was 12 years ago because lenders are that much more structured and knowledgeable.

What have you learnt from working with the Japanese?
Japanese are quality-focused, hard working, and honest people. I have learnt a lot from the Japanese on quality.

Is getting skilled people an issue?
We have problems in getting the right kind of people, for sure. Our acceptance rate is as low as 1 per cent—out of 100 people we interview, we accept one. It's a real challenge. The quality of ITI (Industrial Training Institute) education is really poor in India. It's a big sham. After passing out of ITI, candidates can't even answer two questions. That's why we have our own entrance test and selection criteria, and we train people until it becomes a way of life; it has paid off.

What was the turning point in your business?

It was just perseverance, plugging away at it day on day, week on week, month on month, and then suddenly we found that we did not have to go after every customer to convince him to buy our machines.

23

Tejas Networks Ltd

'In technology, you never miss the boat'
Sanjay Nayak

TEJAS NETWORKS LTD

Founder: Sanjay Nayak

Year of founding: 2000

Headquarters: Bangalore

Website: tejasnetworks.com

Area of business: Telecommunications
networking products

Revenue: $150 million in FY09
(₹2,700 crore cumulative since start-up)

Profit: Not disclosed

Uniqueness

*Aims to offer software-driven networking hardware that
is flexible as networks get upgraded to the next generation
and user profiles change and get more data intensive. Has
'converted a hardware problem into a software problem'.*

By Sridhar K. Chari

It is better to have a small piece of a large pie than vice versa, believes
Sanjay Nayak, and no, he is not talking about a cautious, risk-averse
approach to entrepreneurship, where you play it safe by going for the
easy pickings.

Rather, the chief executive officer and managing director of Tejas
Networks Ltd, an oft-cited example of a successful technology product maker, is simultaneously talking about two different decisions
that are at the heart of any start-up: How much ownership should
you give up in return for crucial funding? And second, which market
will you compete in?

'You have to be well-funded. Not ensuring that is a mistake that a
lot of entrepreneurs make,' Nayak says. 'Don't worry about giving up
too much to bring in more money. Take more money than you need,
and take money when you don't need money. Better to have a small
piece of a large pie than a large piece of a small pie.'

Nayak is a first-generation entrepreneur. As he puts it, 'I was a usual guy, studied in India, then went to the US, etc.' He went on to 'do' the Indian operations of two large multinationals. After stints at Cadence Design Systems Inc. and Synopsys Inc., where he served as India head, the ideating began in earnest.

'All through my career I was a products man. So I thought, hey, we don't have a product company in India? Then we thought, which domain? Having spent my life till then in VLSI (very large scale integrated circuits), electronic design automation and the allied software domain, that was one natural thing to consider. But then we thought, that industry is $5 billion worldwide. If we start a company, we should take it on a big scale, go global. Why not telecom? That was a $250 billion market.'

Clearly, he likes large pies.

Optical products were chosen because they were 'future proof', heralding the driving theme of Tejas—getting 'future ready, today.'

Today, Tejas is moving to grab a greater share of telecommunications operators' spending on network capital expenditure.

A great team is important too, and Nayak went about building one. Arnob Roy, his former colleague from Synopsys, is chief technology officer (CTO) at Tejas. Then, there is Kumar Sivarajan from the Indian Institute of Science (IISc), who wrote a book on optical networking and was introduced to Tejas by entrepreneurial guru Desh Deshpande, mentor and guide to Nayak.

The use of a network drives a lot of innovation, Nayak points out. 'In the US, all the optical networks were built to high capacity after the Internet boom at the turn of the century. It got consumed till 2007 at a certain pace. Then the iPhone happened. It was introduced by AT&T and in 30 months, data traffic grew by 5,000 per cent.'

The other key factors in the business include the technology itself, and then standardization. After all, networks have to talk to each other.

'So you have to track technology, standards, and usage. For a product company, the challenge is to put this together with a secret sauce. The view that finally wins is what the customer wants,' says

Nayak. 'That is what is exciting about being a product company in this space. There is no dearth of excitement, it is a continual optimization process.'

But the 'good news', as he puts it, is that the technological change itself presents exciting opportunities to jump into the market midstream. 'In technology, you never miss the boat. You can catch the next one. Something else is always coming up. The faster the rate of change of technology, the better it is for Indian companies. That is at the core of the next generation of tech companies that will be built in India.'

What Tejas has done, he says, is take the research and development (R&D) cost advantage in India and leverage it in several ways. 'If something requires $100 million to execute in the US, you can do it in $25 million (in India). This is disruptive. So you can do more ideas for the same cost, and increase the probability of winning ideas. Or you can do more R&D and capture a greater part of the value chain. Or you can decrease the time-to-market. Collectively, this is what I call the innovation leverage, which is more than just the labour arbitrage, which the IT services people did. We still invest a lot in R&D.'

With a cumulative revenue of ₹2,700 crore or so since starting up, and profitable since financial year 2008, Nayak believes the next inflection point will push Tejas towards becoming a $1 billion company, grabbing at least 40-50 per cent of network capital expenditure spending, from 10 per cent today.

A key speciality of Tejas is how it has converted a hardware problem into a software one, he says, leveraging a key strength of Indian talent.

'We have continually been among the first in the world to offer products that seamlessly transition a network from voice to mixed to data-centric. Our products allowed operators to do that without changing the box, by only upgrading software.'

The best years are yet to come, he believes. 'Chinese companies like Huawei are becoming strong, while Western companies are struggling too much financially to be able to do much R&D,' Nayak says.

What is more, big spending is expected in India, both in the optical space and beyond. The government is aiming for broadband connectivity to interior areas, defence is planning a nationwide network for not only traditional communications, command and control, but for electronic defence and warfare, and even a 'national knowledge network' is being envisioned.

'There is huge opportunity,' Nayak says.

Q&A
SANJAY NAYAK

Looking back on the journey, what inflection points would you identify?

The first milestone is when you get the sense that you are past infant mortality. Very crucial in any start-up. When we began in 2000, there was the economic downturn and then 9/11. The world was collapsing and India was not a market. But in hindsight it was the best time to start as nobody was bothered about technology, but on fixing what was broken.

Then the Tatas became our first client. It answered the question, could we build a product and would a customer buy from us, when they could buy from established best-in-class? Do we have a compelling enough value proposition, and can you sell it?

After that comes the steady scaling. And in 2007, we innovated with a new business model, where in partnership with Nortel, now Ciena, we could sell across the globe. The technology was ours, the badging, sales and marketing was theirs. It made sense to them, as they could in turn focus their technology on a different end of the market.

Now we are heading to the third inflection point. Tejas 3.0, where we will go for a larger share of the network spend beyond just optical products, which should take us past the $1 billion mark.

What was your technological differentiator?

We converted a hardware problem into a software problem. When operators move from one generation network to the next and usage patterns change, with our 'boxes' they can just upgrade the software. The obsolescence cycle is seven years in telecom. You can't have a box going out of date in two years. With our products, operators could go from a 95-5 voice and data mix to 50-50 to eventually say 80-20.

What are the factors in an entrepreneur's success?

Number one is passion. You have to believe in what you are doing and enjoy doing it, and be committed to that cause. That is the most important thing.

If you are an entrepreneur for any other reason—making money, etc.—that is transitional, and will not help you stay the course.

The second thing is the team. If you have to do anything of scale and size, on a world-class level, you need a world-class team, across the ranks, functions, with complementary skill sets, with different viewpoints, even passionately disagreeing, with one another.

The third thing is to be well-funded.

Lastly, a lot of people get timed out. The idea is good, execution is fine, but do you have the lasting power? No point if you are not there at the table when the big meal is served, because you left too soon!

What kind of entrepreneurial ecosystem do you see around you?

It is changing. We need to create IPR (intellectual property rights) and there should be more product ideas. I am starting to see that coming into play. Second, venture capital funding availability is improving; even early stage is getting better. Media is now paying more attention to start-ups and even the government is realizing that the next phase of economic growth will come from not just mega corporations but small entrepreneurships.

On the negative side, from a societal perspective, there are not enough people willing to come out of their comfort zone and take the plunge. The tech workforces are coming from a middle-class background, and a side effect of global MNCs (multinational corporations) coming here is that there is a sense of 'Life is good, why should I leave this?' that is holding things back. They need to be more restless. And even as a society, we are not yet mature enough to celebrate failure.

24

Tirumala Milk Products (P) Ltd

'Farmers vote for us every day'
B. Brahma Naidu

TIRUMALA MILK PRODUCTS (P) LTD

Founders: B. Brahma Naidu, V. Nageswara Rao,
N. Venkata Rao and D. Brahmanandam

Year of founding: 1995

Headquarters: Hyderabad

Website: www.tirumalamilkproducts.com

Area of business: Dairy products

Revenue: ₹1,200 crore in 2010–11

Profit: Not disclosed

Uniqueness

*Tirumala Milk Products draws its strength from the
thousands of farmers who supply it with milk every day,
its state-of-the-art processing equipment, and a strong sales
and distribution network in Andhra Pradesh and parts
of Tamil Nadu and Karnataka. A fast-growing dairy, it
has scaled up operations to identify opportunities in new
markets and aggressively works on its product portfolio in
line with market demand.*

By Yogendra Kalavalapalli

When a renowned private equity firm like the Carlyle Group LP
invested $22 million (about ₹110 crore) in a hitherto unknown milk
producer in May 2010, it took many by surprise.

What promise did the private equity firm, ranked third globally
in 2011 by London-based Private Equity International (PEI), see in
Tirumala Mik Products (P) Ltd, a company that operates mostly out
of the interior districts of Andhra Pradesh?

For one thing, milk production in India, the world's largest producer, is forecast to grow 3 per cent yearly to 153 million tonnes (mt)
or 37.7 per cent by 2020, according to an agricultural outlook report
prepared by the Organization for Economic Co-operation and Development and the Food and Agriculture Organization. Figures with

the National Dairy Development Board of India show milk production in the country doubled from 55.7 mt in 1991–92 to 112.5 mt
in 2009–10.

And in a highly competitive market like Andhra Pradesh, the second-largest milk producer in the country, the rise of Tirumala Mik
Products in a market of 102 dairies is perhaps worth a B-school case
study.

Tirumala Milk Products started as an intermediary (providing
10,000 litres of chilled milk every day) in the supply chain of a small
dairy in a village and has become a top producer with a considerable
market share in Andhra Pradesh, Tamil Nadu, and Karnataka, producing 1.3 million litres of milk a day. In Andhra Pradesh alone, it
has a 9 per cent market share.

Managing director and co-founder Bolla Brahma Naidu is the son
of a small farmer who owned about three acres in a village in Guntur
district. Naidu speaks only Telugu and prefers dressing in khadis as
white as the milk he supplies to thousands of households every day.
Ask him if language isn't a barrier in these times and he counters,
'The Chinese can't speak English as well. But isn't the world running after them?'

Naidu spent his childhood helping the family take care of the farm
and tending to the livestock. This was where he picked up the skills
that would later help him build a ₹1,200 crore empire. Despite his
professed lack of interest in education, he had an entrepreneurial
streak that he nurtured. Plunging headlong into building something
of his own meant he learnt things the hard way.

After the economic liberalization of the early 1990s, the dairy
business boomed in India, especially so in Andhra Pradesh where
a number of dairies, both cooperatives and private, sprang up. The
dairies would get milk from thousands of farmers, then process,
package, and distribute it in towns and cities.

This was a three-step process. Every day, a farmer would milk his
buffalo or cow and drop the unprocessed milk off at a collection
point in the village, from where it would be taken to a chilling centre

located nearby. The milk would be cooled to increase its life and transported to a dairy.

Naidu and his partner-friends set up a chilling centre in Vella-lacheruvu village of Prakasam district with an investment of ₹30 lakh that they had raised in their personal capacities. They would chill 10,000 litres of milk every day and supply it to a local dairy they were affiliated to. The dairy would pay for the milk, which they would in turn disburse to the farmers after deducting their share.

A year into their venture, just as they were finding their feet in the business, came a blow. Ravileela Dairy, to which they were supplying chilled milk, had run into trouble and defaulted on payments. The amount totalled ₹40 lakh, which included money that had to be paid to farmers who supplied them milk. 'To clear this outstanding amount, we had to raise a ₹22 lakh loan from the Andhra Pradesh State Finance Corporation,' Naidu says. This won Naidu and his partners considerable goodwill among the villagers.

Tirumala Mik Products now had to find a dairy that would take its milk. That buyer was Heritage Foods India Ltd, managed by the family of former Andhra Pradesh chief minister N. Chandrababu Naidu. But that deal also unexpectedly came to an end.

By then the company was handling 40,000 litres a day. 'Milk is a perishable product and if your milk has no takers for that day, it is wasted,' says Naidu. As the milk kept pouring in from farmers, Naidu and his team had to find a dairy that would buy it, and quickly. 'We were caught in between. We couldn't stop procuring milk from farmers and at the same time, there was no one to buy the milk.'

The city of Chennai, which the company ventured into in 1998, proved to be the turning point. One of the partners, Danda Brahmanandam, a professional with experience in the dairy industry before he joined up with Naidu, relocated to the Tamil Nadu capital. A small shed was rented to set up a packaging station and operations were launched.

From distributing 10,000 litres a day in the first month, the demand for Thirumala Milk (the brand name had to be changed in line with the Tamil pronunciation) grew to 20,000 litres in two

Q&A (translated from Telugu)
B. BRAHMA NAIDU

How have you all been able to work together as partners and friends all these years?
We are more friends than business partners who have known each other for a long time, from even before we set up the business. We arrive at a decision together and discuss everything before we go public and work on our plans. There are no egos among us. We do everything together. From cycles to a motorcycle, jeep and cars, we bought everything together. Initially, when we bought a jeep, we used to share it between our families. We were friends from the time we went around on bicycles. We are strongly attached to our roots; we still remember our days as friends before we became business partners. We suffered together, cried and supported each other in times of adversity, and built this company together.

What advantage do you have over your competitors?
If you take some of the other big dairies, the implementation of ideas takes a lot of time. Even a small decision needs several approvals and there is lot of hierarchy... In our case, if I have an idea, all four of us (the founders) meet up or call each other and deliberate at length before we reach a decision. Once we take a decision, we work on implementing it immediately. That is very important. It gives us an edge over our competitors. For example, we reached a decision to set up a tetrapak (packaging) machine in one hour.

What were the struggles you faced along the way?
Coming from farmers' families, we had no godfathers in the dairy industry. We came up through hard work alone and have reached this position after many struggles. If you observe the big dairies in this part of the country, (they) are owned by top politicians. We withstood competition from bigger dairies and yet emerged successful in this market. We faced many risks along the way. There were days when we wanted to quit this industry, unable to take the pressure anymore. We would wonder if we could get out of our debts. We never resorted to short cuts. We believed in hard work and it is our only asset.

169

Is language a barrier?

The Chinese can't speak English well. But isn't the world running after them? Just because I can't speak English doesn't mean I don't have knowledge. Relationship with farmers is the most crucial aspect in this industry. They speak Telugu and I speak in Telugu, which is more important. Besides, my partners are well-educated and can converse well in English. I recently received an agri-business award in Mumbai. Even there I addressed the gathering in Telugu, which someone translated. It is my determination, self belief, and courage that have stood me in good stead.

What is your advice to aspiring entrepreneurs?

Any entrepreneur should have sound knowledge of the industry he is planning to enter. That is very important. Only after having complete facts should one set up business. This is crucial to succeed in any business. For example, if someone wants to set up a dairy plant, he/she should work in the dairy industry for sometime, learn how the business operates, and assess the pros and cons before going ahead.

25

Trivitron Group of Companies

G.S.K. Velu

TRIVITRON GROUP OF COMPANIES

Founder: G.S.K. Velu

Year of founding: 1997

Headquarters: Chennai

Website: www.trivitron.com

Area of business: Medical equipments

Revenue: ₹400 crore

Profit: Not disclosed

Uniqueness

Trivitron has early mover advantage in manufacturing diagnostic and implants which will help it become a leader. The international joint ventures will grow its capabilities and gain a footing in the medical devices and equipments market.

By Bridget Leena

When Gomathy Sachidananda Kulandi Velu chose a job twenty three years ago with a medical devices company over a better paying job as a pharmaceutical salesman, he had no way of knowing his first employer would inspire his future stint as an entrepreneur.

Today, the fast-talking 42-year-old heads the Trivitron group of companies spanning 15 medical specialties over 400 products and present in 15 cities across India. The group, which started in 1997 with an investment of ₹20 lakh, expects to close this fiscal with ₹500 crore of revenue.

Trivitron, which makes laboratory diagnostic and other healthcare equipment, implants, and medical devices, is also present in Sri Lanka, West Asia, and South Africa and plans to expand to South-East Asia and other parts of South Asia.

In 1988, when Velu graduated with a bachelor's degree in pharmacy specializing in bio-medical engineering from Birla Institute of Technology and Science (BITS) in Pilani, Rajasthan, he had two job offers. One was from a pharmaceutical company to be a medical representative at a salary of ₹7,100 a month, triple the offer from IMI Medical Pvt. Ltd, a medical device distributor.

Yet Velu, whose father was a librarian and whose mother pawned her jewellery to educate him, allowed his deep-seated interest in medical devices, stoked by images of unused imported machinery during a hospital internship, to override the salary premium that could have helped him tide over financial difficulties.

'I always took risks and never went after money,' says Velu in an interview at his office in central Chennai.

Initially, Velu, like most domestic medical device sellers, leaned on trading imported machinery to Indian medical establishments, but found that a sales uptick often motivated overseas suppliers to set up their own office in India and snap ties with Velu's distribution service.

'You need to manufacture to survive,' Velu explains.

One of the earliest lessons Velu says he learnt was to move forward without becoming bitter or distraught.

DEER IN A FOREST

Having studied in a Tamil-medium government school in a small village called Arulvahimozhi close to the southern-most tip of Tamil Nadu, Velu didn't let his uneven English proficiency at the time block his dream of becoming a doctor.

But that dream crashed and even though he is nonchalant today about missing the chance to study medicine by a whisker despite scoring 97 per cent in school, it was undeniably devastating for him as a 16-year-old. A disappointed Velu opted for the other obvious option of engineering, but within months realized that it wasn't his calling and opted for admission to the BITS, Pilani course.

'You have to be like the deer in the forest... You have to keep running,' Velu emphasizes.

His first chance to showcase his animal spirits came in the face of a crisis in his first job.

One day, his boss at IMI Medical showed him a letter from American diagnostics major Ciba Corning threatening to terminate its contract with IMI's services unit Allied Healthcare if it did not do a certain level of business that year. Allied Healthcare had fallen off the radar for IMI.

Velu jumped in to revive the fraying fortunes of the unit.

Soon, the business experienced not just a revival but surpassed expectations by logging more revenue than the parent company. Impressed with the phenomenal growth, his boss made the then 21-year-old Velu a partner.

Allied grew rapidly and eventually started earning more revenue than IMI, which was run by his boss.

BRANCHING OUT

Differences arose and widened between Velu and other IMI partners; he quit the company in 1992 to head American biotechnology company Chiron Corp.'s India operations. Swiss pharmaceutical company Novartis International AG acquired Chiron in 2006.

'It was a tough and painful decision to leave my (late) boss and Allied Healthcare, which I painstakingly rebuilt,' says Velu.

At Chiron he learnt the importance of long-term planning, which he says forms the essence of several American firms.

'Without a vision you cannot create a large enterprise, you create only a mom and pop store,' Velu says.

While working for a multinational had its advantages, Velu began to itch to start something on his own, with constant nudging from his mentor N.P.V. Ramasamy Udayar, founder of Sri Ramachandra Medical College and Research Institute.

Trivitron Medical System was set up in 1997.

Without the support of 'Udayar uncle' and Apollo Hospitals Enterprise Ltd founder Prathap Reddy, he couldn't have started out on his own to compete with multinationals such as Siemens AG and Roche Holding AG, Velu says.

Crisis struck early. In 1999, a distribution order worth ₹15 crore was cancelled, pushing the company towards bankruptcy and shrinking its employee size from 25 to 10. But Velu's newly formed diagnostic lab business turned out to be a lifesaver.

FALL BACK OPTIONS

'You have to be on more than one project at a time,' says Velu. 'If you are working on 10 things and three of them fail, you have backups. But if you focus on a single venture then there's nothing for you to lean back on in times of failure.'

The company was ready to grow inorganically through acquisitions. In 2000, his Metropolis Health Services India Ltd acquired Sudharama Diagnostics and in 2001 it took over Lister Diagnostics. From one lab in Mumbai, the diagnostic business has now expanded to 75 centres in India with revenue of ₹350 crore.

'We are constantly looking out for tie-ups as we believe in the partnership model,' Velu says.

Metropolis expanded operations to Sri Lanka and Dubai to boost revenue from laboratory tests overseas that was ten times more than what it earned from referral laboratories in India.

'I learnt to build a business of scale after working in multinationals,' he says.

In 2007, HSBC Private Equity and venture capital firm ePlanet Ventures bought a minority stake for $11 million (about ₹ 55 crore) in Trivitron. The private equity investments gave the required impetus to set up an indigenous manufacturing facility in Sriperumbudur near Chennai. Trivitron also has seven international joint ventures to manufacture medical devices.

In 2010, the company commissioned Trivitron Medical Technology Park that expects 10 factories to invest ₹250 crore, allowing the first phase of the project to be completed by 2012–15.

The setting up of Trivitron group and its lab testing business Metropolis Health Services India Ltd has not satiated Velu entrepreneurial thirst. He is the founder of two other initiatives in the healthcare space—Medfort Hospitals, a network of diabetes and vision care hospitals, and Alliance Medicorp, a chain of dialysis and dental care institutions.

Has Velu achieved what he set out to do as a young entrepreneur two decades ago?

'I have just scratched the surface, there is more to achieve,' he replies with a twinkle in his eyes.

Q&A
G.S.K. VELU

If you had to attribute your success to one person who would it be?
There is no one person. It starts with my mother who sold her last piece of gold jewellery to see me graduate. Ravindran, my first boss, I consider him a mentor from whom I learnt about medical devices. N.P.V. Ramasamy Udayar—founder of Sri Ramachandra Medical College and Research Institute, a mentor to do multiple initiatives in the healthcare space and also supported me to become an entrepreneur.

What are the lessons learnt from working for a multinational Ciba Corning which you would not have learnt working for an Indian company?
Have a vision and think big. I have learnt to run my business in a professional manner and not bring in family members as then my excellent team will not be able do their work. Nearly seven of my top management members have been with from the inception of Trivitron. Just choose the right set of people to work with.

Why is India lagging behind in medical technology space? What is required?
India still does not have a specific ministry to promote the medical technology industry; it neither belongs to health, family and welfare ministry nor the chemical and fertilizer ministry. Neither do we come under the ambit of the science and technology.

The environment for manufacturing devices is not conducive as the excise duties are higher for imported raw material or components than the imported finished medical devices.

Today there are ten Chinese multinationals with more than $1 billion market capitalization and India today is where China was 15–16 years ago.

177

Why does India need to have own manufacturing medical technology space?
Being a populist country, we cannot hugely be dependent on imports. Secondly, we have large capability for doing clinical research which others do not have.

When we have the patients and problems why do we need to import kits and equipments from overseas? We still do not have India normal rate for diabetes or blood pressure and follow other countries.

What is your word of motivation for young entrepreneurs?
Be passionate about what you want to do and taking risks is part of being an entrepreneur. Become an entrepreneur in the field where you have domain knowledge.

26

TVS Logistics Services Ltd

Living up to a legacy
R. Dinesh

TVS LOGISTICS SERVICES LTD

Founder: R. Dinesh*

Year of founding: 2004

Headquarters: Chennai

Website: www.tvslogisticsservices.com

Area of business: Logistics solutions

Revenue: ₹1,350 crore in 2010–11

Profit: ₹60-70 crore profit before taxes in 2010–11

Uniqueness

TVS Logistics has differentiated itself by taking ownership of goods from various component makers and delivering them directly to the vehicle manufacturers, saving them the cost, time and effort needed to deal with each individual shipment.

By Vidya Padmanabhan

R. Dinesh's future had been charted out for him at birth. Like his three siblings and numerous other members of the extended TVS family, he knew at an early age that his destiny lay in the illustrious automotive conglomerate started by his great grandfather.

With that security, he could have coasted on the many successes of TV Sundram Iyengar and Sons Ltd. Instead, he was prompted to think a little differently by an adviser, Harvard Business School professor Tarun Khanna, who told him, 'You have a choice: do you want to live off the brand, or do want to build the brand?'

Dinesh chose to build the brand—not by growing the well-established businesses of the TVS group, but by stewarding a new line of business and building it into a separate successful company, TVS Logistics Services Ltd.

The company, which began as a TVS business unit in 1997 with just ₹20 lakh as capital, provides end-to-end logistics services with a

---

*The company started as a unit of TV Sundram Iyengar and Sons Ltd

focus on the mobility segment—including cars, commercial vehicles, off-road vehicles, defence vehicles, and construction equipment. Incorporated in 2004, when it had a ₹70-crore turnover, the company will earn revenue of ₹1,850 crore in 2011-12, according to Dinesh.

'We have been growing at a 40 per cent CAGR,' Dinesh says. 'The other big satisfaction is that we created a unique model that I think most Indian companies have struggled to develop. We are the only Indian logistics multinational.'

With logistics costs forming a significant portion of a nation's gross domestic product—the Indian market is estimated at $200 billion by 2020—Dinesh sees great potential for his company. In the automotive sector on which TVS Logistics focuses, the company is the market leader in India with an estimated 9-10 per cent market share, according to Dinesh. Globally, the company is as yet a 'minuscule player' even in its chosen sectors, but has big plans, he says.

Born in Madurai—where the TVS group has its origins—into the fourth generation of the sprawling TVS family, Dinesh dropped out of an undergraduate engineering programme to study chartered accountancy, for which he had greater aptitude. That grounding in finance has stood him in good stead as the head of a company, the tall, loose-limbed 46-year-old says, but he didn't get to hone those skills during his first decade in the TVS group, as he worked his way through the long apprenticeship that the group puts even its family members through.

TVS Logistics began as an experiment, Dinesh says. In the mid 1990s, he had set up a warehouse in Madurai for the TVS group's auto-part distribution business, along the lines of those he had seen in the UK and other countries. The concept had significantly increased the availability of components and reduced the need for inventory for companies overseas, and Dinesh hoped to produce the same effect for the TVS group, which had previously stored stock at several locations.

The idea to offer the warehousing solutions to third parties came from an auto industry veteran, S. Ravichandran, who had just joined the TVS Group, and is now the president of TVS Logistics.

'He came and said, "Why don't we look at logistics as (a) separate business?",' Dinesh says. 'All businesses that TVS is in had a logistics component. Distribution was one of the core activities of the company. Logistics was something we thought we could support for third parties.'

The logistics unit got started in 1997 as one of the ventures of the projects division, which Dinesh had set up to help the group test the waters in new businesses.

Making the first few sales were tough, Dinesh says, and the TVS group, with its tantalizing volume of business within arm's reach, did not help. 'Just like everywhere else, the group was the hardest to crack,' Dinesh says. To ensure that the business succeeded on its own merits, Dinesh and his team had to look outside the group. Even today, group business contributes only 15 per cent of the company's revenue.

It took many pitches before the company got any business, according to Dinesh. 'Ravi and I would go and meet customers, and they would say, "This concept won't work in India. People are not going to have a common warehouse or outsource their warehouse".' But the team persisted, inviting prospective customers to tour the warehouse. Soon, the earthmoving equipment maker JCB became a client, and in a little more than a year, business was in full swing.

In 2004, Dinesh began looking overseas. 'I wanted to buy a company in the UK because we had a choice—whether we would go with our customers overseas, or we would just stay with the Indian logistics market,' he says. 'So we said we would go with our customers because that model is unique, rather than stay local as a typical logistics player.'

The acquisition proposal prompted the board of TVS and Sons in 2004 to hive off the logistics business, with a turnover of ₹70 crore at that point, into a separate company, with no extra capital—only a transfer of assets from the business unit to the company.

The 'shoestring budget' worked in the company's favour, Dinesh says. 'We never had a chance to look at something big. Maybe because of that, as well as our typical mindset, we never invested in assets. But that stood us in very good stead when we realized later on, looking at research and analyzing how companies had grown globally, companies that had invested a lot in fixed assets had struggled to get good returns.'

Instead of buying up warehouses, trucks, ships, and ports—TVS Logistics leases them. 'Even the larger companies have moved to this mode—where they own assets only where it's required,' Dinesh says.

The company also sets itself apart by providing material management services rather than just moving consignments around. TVS Logistics takes ownership of goods and delivers them directly into the production line at the receiving end, a unique practice.

The model made sense for vehicle manufacturers that would rather deal with one large supplier than 20 small ones. And it also made sense for component makers who didn't have such large orders from each customer to justify doing everything on their own, Dinesh says. Customers grew to use TVS Logistics as their extended arm, and in the process, the company became integral to their supply chain.

With plans to expand globally, and eventually list the company to fund the expansion, Dinesh decided to look outside the TVS Group for funds. In 2008, in a first for the group, TVS Logistics received private equity investment of ₹100 crore from Goldman Sachs Capital Partners. '₹100 crore is still small money,' Dinesh says. 'But it gave us a lot of leverage. That meant we could raise another ₹300 crore in debt and things like that.'

When Dinesh took charge of the logistics business unit in 1997, there was no stated aim to go global or be No. 1. The venture was just an attempt to tap into the expertise and relationships TVS had established, Dinesh says, and its runaway success was a pleasant surprise. The company had aimed to grow to ₹1,000 crore by 2012, but reached that target early, in 2010.

The next big milestone for the company is $1 billion in revenue and an initial public offering by 2015.

'Think big,' Dinesh says. 'Not just thinking big for big's sake, but whether it makes sense for that business to do so. And be forearmed as to what pitfalls you might face. I have seen start-ups which grow to have three-four successes, and they believe after this everything will be successful. They forget the lesson that you have to be forearmed.'

Q&A
R. DINESH

What has been a high point for you in the TVS Logistics journey?
The real high point was the acquisition of Multipart (Holding) in the UK in 2004. That transformed us from being a small Indian logistics company trying to become global to a company that had a UK corporate office, which could reach out to the whole of Europe. That was the real big point.

You've said 'Think big'. Any other lessons for budding entrepreneurs?
One thing I learnt very quickly—not only in logistics but also one or two businesses that I started, some of which failed, but some of which did very well—I wouldn't say there is a single success mantra that works across all businesses. Finally, it's about how well you execute, and without people you are just not going to execute. When people ask me (for advice), there's only one thing I tell them: 'Empower your people. If you think you know better than them, then we have a problem.'

One learning from those failed businesses?
There has to be something unique in your business model. You cannot say, 'I will do the same thing as someone else, and just because I'm a brand, I will succeed.' It can be a very small differentiator, but the differentiator must be there.

Being a part of the TVS family, has it been a support in your entrepreneurial journey, or a source of pressure to succeed?
I've used the TVS reputation and relevance to gain access to customers and people. But there is definitely a pressure that I cannot 'ruin' or (damage) the brand, which I think is good. No complaints on that score. I've enjoyed the pressure. The good and the bad even out.

What are some of the challenges your business has faced?
Profitability. When you're a start-up trying to grow, a significant element of the cost you have to incur is the marketing cost. And second is the people. The

top rung you may be able to get, but suddenly when you have to grow from 1,000 persons to 8,000 people, it's a big challenge. We have struggled to find the right talent at the No. 2, No. 3 levels. The main challenge has been to make people think global, and not just about the local customers.

27

Updater Services Ltd

The pioneer in facilities management
T. Raghunandana

UPDATER SERVICES LTD

Founder: T. Raghunandana
Year of founding: 1985
Headquarters: Chennai
Website: www.uds.in
Area of business: Facilities management services
Revenue: More than ₹300 crore
Profit: Not disclosed

Uniqueness

*India's largest facilities management services company,
looking at acquisitions for growth and to expand its
presence in the western parts of the country.*

By S. Bridget Leena

T. Raghunandana has built the 26-year-old Updater Services Ltd into India's largest facilities management company, with an army of blue-collar employees to offer equipment maintenance, water and waste management, pest control, and catering services for factories, airports, and offices.

Raghunandana, a reluctant interviewee, is modest about his accomplishment in scaling up the company into a ₹300 crore business. It began with two employees and now has a headcount of 30,000 people.

'A lot of thought did not go into the business and the investment was very meagre,' he says about the beginnings of the company.

He does accept that until Updater came along, services related to managing company sites were largely available on a piecemeal basis and done by workers such as plumbers and electricians.

Prior to starting Updater, Raghunandana tried his hand at running a brick kiln. This was soon after he graduated with a bachelor's degree in accounting and finance from Guru Nanak College in Chennai.

The Indian Navy was setting up a base in Arakkonam, 70 km from Chennai and close to his ancestral land, and he saw a business opportunity for newly baked bricks. But he sold the kiln as making bricks didn't seem to be his calling in life.

'I realized I was not cut out for manufacturing—it did not offer flexibility of a service industry, to scale up or trim the business depending on the demand,' he says.

A trip to Europe in the early 1980s provided the inspiration for Updater Services. During his travel, a young Raghunandana observed European airports and offices being maintained by facilities management companies, a concept then unheard of in India.

In 1985, he employed two people and started operating Updater Services from a room at his Mylapore home in central Chennai.

For more than a decade after he started the business, Updater seemed to be an idea whose time had still not come.

It was only in 2000 that facilities management services acquired scale with the growth of the information technology sector and increasing demand for standardized services related to the maintenance of machinery, office cleaning, and catering.

Around the same time, Chennai-based Tidel Park, one of the largest information technology parks in Asia, hired Updater as a facilities manager. This contract proved to be path-breaking for Raghunandana, who went on to win yet another prestigious project— that of managing Hitec city in Hyderabad.

As Updater cemented its place as India's largest facilities management service in terms of manpower and square footage being managed, it attracted private equity investment in 2006 from New Vernon Bharat that bought a 40 per cent stake in the company for ₹40 crore. But when New Vernon Bharat sold that stake to ICICI Ventures for ₹100 crore in 2008, Raghunandana bitterly rued his hasty decision to sell such a large stake.

Today, the company manages the offices of top Indian as well as overseas businesses including Infosys Ltd, State Bank of India, and Hyundai Motor India Ltd.

'Our job is to maintain things in a way that we know when a particular equipment is going to fail and so we don't need to give reasons for any breakdown unless, of course, there's an earthquake or something... That is the level of service agreement,' Raghunandana says.

The company has 'never lost business because we've goofed up', he says.

Updater employees ensure that airport floors and toilets in Delhi, Bangalore, and Hyderabad are spotless. Its workforce is deployed in maintaining backup power equipment and factory machinery, making sure every widget in the manufacturing process functions smoothly.

There are challenges. Rising industrialization has increased labour costs, shrinking margins from 25 per cent to 10 per cent, and spurred attrition. Valuable employees trained in plumbing or electrical work are quick to move on to more lucrative jobs.

Raghunandana admits that it is tough to recruit people and retain them.

The founder of Updater Services is involved in multiple social initiatives to equip people with the required skills and build an employable workforce. The company has teamed up with self-help groups in Tamil Nadu to offer vocational training for women.

Raghunandana has also partnered with PanIIT—an alumni group covering all the Indian Institutes of Technology—and started a school to train welders and housekeepers near Chengalpattu, 30 km south of Chennai. The centre trains 100 workers every month, who are then recruited by Updater Services.

'People are very important,' Raghunandana says, adding that food and residential facilities are what will attract rural people to work in the cities. 'Otherwise, why should he or she leave the comfort of the home and village?'

Raghunandana's interest in people management is also reflected in the welfare benefits that he offers his employees—he covers all of them with 24-hour personal accident insurance instead of just restricting it to work hours.

After being largely information technology-focused, Raghunandana has diversified and sought business from other sectors, servicing airports, factories of glass maker Saint Gobain Glass India, and Apollo and Wockhardt hospitals.

As a result, the company was shielded from the negative impact of the financial crisis three years ago on the information technology sector.

Raghunandana is eyeing ₹1,000 crore of revenue by expanding across India—65 per cent of his business comes from the south—and is considering acquisitions of ₹30-40 crore to make a dent in markets close to Mumbai.

Q&A
T. RAGHUNANDANA

What difference has Updater made to the facilities management segment?
In 1985 when I started out, the concept was unheard of in the country although individuals such as electricians or plumbers would offer their services largely for residences. We are the pioneers of making facilities management services into an organized business. It is still a fragmented business.

Are private equity investors showing interest? Where do you see Updater in three years?
Yes, private equity firms evince interest, but currently I do not plan to tap them. Our turnover should grow to ₹1,000 crore. We are growing at 15 per cent every year without adding new customers. This is largely due to scaling up of salaries every year by 15 per cent. We are also actively scouting for acquisitions in Mumbai, Pune, and Ahmedabad to strengthen our presence in those parts of the country.

Where is the next growth area for facilities management services?
(I am) yet to see any visible signs so far in the country. I feel growth for facilities management will happen for integrated townships when there are more such townships coming up, and slowly even large residential developments housing over 100 apartments will witness it. This has already been seen in Western countries.

Do different facilities require different set services?
For example, we offer services for both Infosys and Apollo Hospitals. In case of a software company, (the focus) would be cleanliness while in the case of healthcare it would be hygiene. Delhi airport would require strict security measures.

If you want to give a word of advice to people starting out as entrepreneurs, what would it be?
Honestly speaking, I don't think I would want to give any advice. But I feel 'You can make money without being evil' is important and everything else like passion and hard work will follow suit.

28

Vasan Healthcare Pvt. Ltd

One order of eye-care to go
A.M. Arun

VASAN HEALTHCARE PVT. LTD

Founder: A.M. Arun

Year of founding: 2001

Headquarters: Chennai

Website: www.vasaneye.in

Area of business: Day-care, primarily eye-care, hospitals

Revenue: ₹500 crore in 2010–11

Profit: ₹100 crore Ebitda in 2010–11

Uniqueness

*The company has several things going for it: a flawed
public healthcare system in India; a willingness to go into
small towns with high demand; the focus on day-care,
thus avoiding high expenditure on the infrastructure
necessary in traditional hospitals.*

By Vidya Padmanabhan

A.M. Arun rejects any attempt to slot Vasan Healthcare Pvt. Ltd,
predominantly a chain of eye-care hospitals, into a frame of reference that includes institutions known for their free eye-camps and
not-for-profit model.

'We are into private healthcare,' the founder and chairman says.
'We want to be very clear—we want to give world-class facilities, the
best of service, world-class doctors, and the eight million people
walking into our clinics should have value for money. That is our
USP (unique selling proposition).'

Arun prefers to step outside the healthcare realm to reach for a
comparison for his chain of day-care hospitals, which provide services
that don't involve overnight stay. 'It's like running a pizza chain,' he
says. 'When McDonald's (Corporation) can have 10,000 stores, we
can have 1,000 hospitals.'

It's a bold association that image consultants might run from, but it comes from a vision that refuses to be clouded by orthodoxy, and one that worked with Sequoia Capital, which has pumped in $50 million in three rounds of private equity investment since 2008.

Vasan Healthcare began as a company in 2001 with one general medicine clinic—the eye-care focus came later—in Tiruchirapalli (Trichy) in Tamil Nadu. A decade later, the group is on track to operate 125 eye-care centres and 25 dental-care clinics around the country by the end of the year, according to Arun, who aims to add 100 clinics a year when the current expansion reaches a steady state.

'We want to be the world's largest healthcare company in the next five years—healthcare company, not just eye-care company.' World domination is possible, he says, because of the health services vacuum in India.

'For a country of 1.2 billion population with no public healthcare system, almost nil, we need more private providers,' he says. 'Who wants to go to a government hospital in India today? And studies say, to take India to the level of developing countries like Indonesia or Thailand, the government has to spend $70-80 billion immediately. That's ₹4 lakh crore. Where is the money? And who's going to provide the service?'

Arun is intensely focused on Vasan, conveying the impression that the sum of the man is his business. But he acknowledges an appreciation for the finer things in life: he collects exclusive brands of watches, shoes, cars, and pens. At 42, having spent his entire working life on his business—he still puts in 16 hours a day at work, and half-days on Sundays—Arun feels he has earned the right to have a Tag Heuer or Rolex tell him when it's time to call it a day.

The Vasan story began in 1947 when Arun's grandfather, leaving his agricultural estates in Malaysia to his elder son, returned to India and bought Vasan Medical Hall, a pharmacy store in Trichy. Arun's father, the younger son, ran the business until his death in 1988, when Arun was in his first year in medical college at Annamalai University in Chidambaram. The first son of the family, Arun felt the need to take charge of affairs, and so, for the next several years, spent four days in college and three days at the business, finally getting his MBBS degree in nine years.

By then, the business bug had bitten hard, and despite his mother's wish for him to get into medical practice, he stayed focused on the business.

Under his stewardship, the medical store that had remained solo for more than four decades expanded to 14 stores in Trichy by 2001. (There are 50 Vasan pharmacy stores across southern Tamil Nadu today.) That year, Arun started a small day-care clinic with three beds, a diagnostic centre, a pharmacy, and 10-12 consultation chambers. He found it did well, and took the model into nearby Thanjavur. In 2003, he set up a multi-speciality 120-bed hospital, and later acquired a 200-bed hospital—ventures that didn't impress him as much.

'I realized multi-speciality was very high-capital,' he says. 'I realized getting the land, building, getting approvals... It was a very complex game. That's why, in India, it takes a very long time to scale up multi-speciality hospitals. We had only one large corporate chain for two or two-and-a-half decades.'

For Arun, all arrows pointed to the day-care model. He zeroed in on eye-care as the one area with the greatest demand, where day-care was feasible. 'Not even large multi-speciality hospitals have a proper ophthalmology department,' he says. 'They are not interested in doing cataract surgery. They are more interested in doing tomo (tomography) work, bypass surgery, just the core of their business. And if you go to a trust hospital, you have to wait in line with hundreds or thousands of people for appointments.'

Once the course was set, Vasan began acquiring local practices to grow to 18 eye-care hospitals by 2008, and, after the fund infusion from Sequoia, set a blistering pace for pan-India expansion.

Though several Vasan centres have come up in recent months in urban areas, the group's focus for growth has been and will remain small towns, Arun says, citing the example of Paramakudi near Madurai. 'It's a tier IV town with less than a lakh (100,000) population.

In that town, we get 150 outpatients per day. People from 60-70 km around Paramakudi come there for treatment. Now, there are 5,000 towns like Paramakudi in this country where Vasan can start.'

There's a reason why large hospitals have not ventured into small towns, and that's talent retention, Arun says. This was a major challenge during Vasan's early days. In its first hospital in Trichy, the company had to put out a dragnet to recruit a junior doctor, and succeeded after eight months. Now, the group's scale has helped it surmount that problem. In Paramakudi, for instance, Vasan now has a doctor on deputation from Delhi.

The group plans to venture into day-care services such as diabetology and fertility treatment next fiscal year, for which it is on the verge of securing $120 million in investment from a sovereign fund. Further expansion will likely be funded by a listing on the stock exchange next fiscal year, if market conditions are favourable, Arun says.

'People always talk about competition in any business in India,' Arun says, exuding confidence about the future of the company. 'But where's the competition in this business? If I wanted to start one more brand in eye-care, I can start another 125 clinics. You can have 10 more Vasan Eyecares at a much larger scale. There's such a huge gap between need and service.'

Q&A
A.M. ARUN

What makes this a good time for Vasan Healthcare?

Look at the per capita income. What was the per capita income in 2001 and what is it today? People are going to spend. People will look at the state of healthcare and they will come to us. It can never fail. Also, the government has started to give insurance schemes—Tamil Nadu has one, Andhra Pradesh has one, Karnataka has one. All this will improve the quality of healthcare from private providers.

Has there been a bleak moment when you doubted what you were doing?

In 2008, when I expanded to 15 hospitals, 10 were fully operational; four-five were yet to be. I didn't have the capital to expand beyond that. All were in newer markets such as Hubli and Kochi. I was thinking, 'Have I made a mistake to get into all these newer markets?' We were losing cash. Credit must go to Sequoia Capital, which stepped in at that moment to give me the capital. That was a bleak moment when I thought I had been more aggressive than I should have been.

Have you felt your lack of a business school education has been a drawback?

We (those without a management degree) tend to commit mistakes while learning—they can be expensive mistakes. On the other hand, we are always on the ground. We tend to know the ground quickly. That helps us quickly grow the business.

What personality traits do you think have helped you succeed in business?

Whatever I've done in my life, I've always wanted perfection. And whatever I undertake, I always think big. As they say, if you aim for the sky, you at least reach the top of the hill. Think big.

Have there been mistakes along the way that you have learnt from?
Mistakes happen every day. I can't think of any major mistakes. I'm aggressive in pursuing expansion for the business. But overall, I've taken baby steps in whatever I do. I always look at the worst that could happen. If things don't go this way, what will happen? If you want to be a success, you should not be very positive. You should always think about what could be the worst.

29

VA Tech Wabag Ltd

The employee who bought the company
Rajiv Mittal

VA TECH WABAG LTD

Founder: Rajiv Mittal

Year of founding: 2005

Headquarters: Chennai

Website: www.wabag.com

Area of business: Water technology

Revenue: ₹734 crore in 2010–11

Profit: ₹55.3 crore in 2010–11

Uniqueness

With lifestyle changes driving higher water consumption in India and other emerging markets, solutions such as desalination will likely be sought after, indicating bright prospects for VA Tech Wabag, which is already building India's largest desalination plant for potable water at Nemmeli, Tamil Nadu.

By Vidya Padmanabhan

Rajiv Mittal's mid-life entrepreneurial journey might never have begun if the right buyer had made a bid when Voest-Alpine Technologie AG was looking to sell its Indian water technology business, which Mittal had established and built up as an employee of the Austrian company.

'We were not very happy with the buyers who were registering their interest,' says Mittal, a chemical engineer who is now the promoter and managing director of the Chennai-based VA Tech Wabag Ltd, a water-management and recycling company with operations in several countries. 'We thought that they would not be in line with successful strategy and growth style we had for the organization in the last seven-eight years. And you can understand the feeling—it was a child I had given birth to. I was the No.1 employee in the business; I was still there. It was more than a job for me.'

And so, along with three other directors of the company, Mittal put in a bid for the company. In 2005, at the age of 45, having never dreamt entrepreneurial dreams, he became part owner of the company he had been serving.

Since then, he hasn't stepped off the gas. Two years after the buyout, VA Tech Wabag India's erstwhile parent, VA Tech Wabag GmbH, was put on the block by the German electronics giant Siemens AG, which had acquired it at the same time Mittal bought the Indian business. The ₹200-crore Chennai-based business ended up acquiring the ₹700-750 crore turnover sprouting Austria-based parent.

'From being a subsidiary of a multinational, we were now an Indian multinational doing a reverse acquisition,' Mittal says. 'I must say that was a great moment for us and for the staff. They got their multinational tag back, and along with that they got the tag of an Indian multinational.'

VA Tech Wabag has implemented more than 6,000 projects—both municipal (involving drinking water processing, sewage treatment, and waste-water treatment) and industrial (such as power plant cooling towers)—around the world. In 2010–11, it made revenue of ₹734 crore.

Mittal's association with his company really began in 1996, when his third employer in the water technology industry, the German company then known as Wabag Kulmbach, sent him from London to Chennai to set up an office and explore opportunities in South-East Asia.

From a ₹9 lakh turnover in its first year, the Chennai unit, led by Mittal, saw a turnover of ₹200 crore in 2004.

'I don't get satisfied by achieving mediocre results,' Mittal says. 'I need to set very high targets. When you succeed, the joy you have, and the pleasure you derive from reaching the targets—it looked impossible but you made it happen—is tremendous.'

By 2004, Voest-Alpine Technologie, which had acquired Wabag in 1999, was losing money in its water businesses in mature markets such as France and Germany, and decided to divest its stake in those units. To make good on its losses, it also decided to sell its profitable Indian business.

'Whichever way life has gone, I have followed it,' Mittal likes to say. 'I have never tried to change the course of life.'

But at least subconsciously, Mittal has lined up a boulder or two to redirect life's course.

When VA Tech Wabag India's potential buyers, some of whom Mittal and his team considered undesirable, asked about the post-buyout career plans of the successful management team, the employees would lay out a list of conditions that would end up deflating the buyers' interest.

A chance conversation during that period with a friend in the finance industry convinced Mittal that he could drum up enough funding support to acquire the company himself. Along with three directors who were 'a bit scared, a bit worried, a bit disbelieving', Mittal put up about 20 per cent finance towards a bid. ICICI Ventures contributed about 65 per cent, debtors put in the rest, and with guarantees from State Bank of India (SBI), the bid of less than ₹100 crore was eventually accepted by the initially dismissive parent.

The euphoria of the moment was quickly tamped down by reality. 'Suddenly we had to look after every month's salary,' Mittal says. 'You have to pay suppliers, contractors. The responsibility comes on to you.' He also had to take care of customers' and employees' concerns about their overnight orphanhood.

SBI's stamp of approval brought other banks' support, and the cash crunch was solved. To assuage customers' concerns, Mittal worked out an agreement with Siemens, by which the Indian company could continue to use Wabag's brand and technology for a period, for a fee. To motivate staff, he gave stock options to all employees.

'It turned out that post-management buyout, our business kept on growing, and kept growing at an almost 40 per cent compounded annual growth rate, which I think nobody expected, and we became a substantial business,' Mittal says.

True to Mittal's belief that success breeds success, more private equity investors came in: GLG Partners Inc. of the UK in 2007, US-based Passport Capital Llc., Hong Kong-based Sattva Investment Advisors Ltd, and the Government of Singapore Investment Corp. Pvt. Ltd (GIC) in 2008.

A listing on the stock exchanges came in 2010, primarily to offer

an exit to investors, apart from demonstrating the company's balance sheet hygiene, thanks to its Teutonic origins, and improving the image of the company. 'If you're a listed company, you're valued very differently,' Mittal says.

Most of the private equity investors cashed in their stakes during the initial public offering—which, even with ₹5 shares priced at ₹1,310, was 36 times oversubscribed. GIC still retains an 8 per cent stake, and Sattva, about 3-4 per cent.

Internationally, VA Tech Wabag counts itself among the top 10 businesses in the highly fragmented water technology market, estimated at $500 billion. Even the top companies—Veolia Water, a unit of French company Veolia Environment SA, and Degremont, a subsidiary of another French company Suez Environment SA—have market shares only in single digits.

The company faces new challenges, Mittal says. It has 20 subsidiaries, most of these inherited from the Wabag acquisition. 'They are all in the most challenging countries—either developing or underdeveloped countries. It's a big challenge to develop local teams, develop trust in them, to empower them, make them accountable, but the control and compliance has to be at the headquarters. We don't want to know too late if something wrong is happening. What is a regular monitoring control mechanism? How do we ensure that corporate guidelines are complied with? That's a big challenge.'

With the central and state governments in India increasingly looking towards the private sector to implement infrastructure projects, Mittal foresees a major role ahead for his company. Private sector participation 'has already happened in telecom, road, power', he says. 'Water is always the last because it's politically so sensitive. But I think in the next Five Year Plan (for 2012–17) that they are going to release, there's going to be a great emphasis on the private sector in water management. We want to be there and we want to take part to retain our leadership.'

— ◈ —

Q&A
RAJIV MITTAL

What is your next big milestone?
Globally, we are within the top ten. Our aim is to be within the top five in the next three-five years. Our target is to reach €1 billion–five times growth– in the next five years. Though the markets are currently not supporting us, our vision has not changed. We may be delayed by one or two years in getting it, but we are adamant about reaching that target.

What is your growth strategy?
We are cash-rich, we are ambitious. Of the €1 billion, almost 75 per cent we plan to have through organic growth, and 25 per cent through inorganic growth. We are continuously looking to acquire international companies.

You like to set high targets. How do you make sure your organization matches your energy?
If you think it, believe it, you work towards it, you will achieve it. That's our mantra. We had a training course in 2006 conducted by ICICI Ventures (a former investor) and were asked to make four affirmations: we'll be a listed company; we'll be a ₹1,000 crore company (in consolidated turnover) with a ₹1,000 crore market capitalization; we will acquire an international company; and we will achieve an export order of $50 million. We just put (this) on everybody's board, everybody's desk, we talked about it. It was like a prayer. Every day, we said, 'We have to get this, we have to get this, we have to get this.' And we got it.

What sets you apart from the competition?
We are a company that is very high-commitment. Clients perceive us as a good, quality-conscious technology company. And we keep ourselves very competitive even though we have tremendous pressure on the employee cost side.

Did you have your family's support when you switched to entrepreneurship?

I'm very independent. My family never objected to it. But I don't think they had any clue of what I was doing and what risk I was taking. The good thing was whatever I did I didn't put my personal assets or securities at risk. I ensured that I didn't do that.

— ◈ —

30
Via

The travel companion
Vinay Gupta

VIA

Founders: Vinay Gupta and Amit Agarwal

Year of founding: 2006

Headquarters: Bangalore .

Website: www.via.com

Area of business: Travel

Revenue: $371 million (gross sales in 2010–11)

Profit: Not disclosed

Uniqueness

Tapping cash commerce by building a network of
more than 20,000 agents and growing.

By Madhurima Nandy

In the summer of 2005, when computer science engineer Vinay Gupta flew back home from the US, he had no clue he was going to build a company of his own, and that too in the travel business, over the next few months. All he knew was that India's economy was booming, offering many business opportunities across industries to entrepreneurs.

In retrospect, it was 'the turning point of my life', Gupta says.

He came back to join a Bangalore-based software company and lost interest after a couple of months and left the job, but not before meeting Amit Agarwal, who worked for the same employer. Over many cups of coffee, the two men discussed multiple business ideas, out of which emerged a plan to set up a travel services company.

First named Flightraja Travels Pvt. Ltd and known today as Via, the Bangalore-based travel firm has built a large offline network with 20,000 agents across 2,400 cities and towns globally, providing an array of travel products including airline, rail and bus tickets, hotel packages, and travel insurance.

Established in July 2006, it also raised funds in its initial days from venture capital investors IndoUS Venture Partners and Sequoia Capital India.

Raising capital wasn't easy, Gupta recalls. Around that time, on-line travel companies had started generating huge interest among investors, with Cleartrip Travel Services Pvt. Ltd and Yatra Online Pvt. Ltd successfully raising funds from investors. 'When we went to investors, the bigger players in the travel space had already raised capital and we were asked what we would do differently,' says Gupta.

Setting up a travel company was not the first and only choice for him and Agarwal. Among many other things, they thought of setting up a real estate portal. However, Gupta says he couldn't understand the revenue model because in India you didn't pay for information, only for transactions.

It took about five-six months of studying research reports and some serious thinking for him to get to the point. 'Travel seemed a more globally scalable product. We knew that once we built a large company, a lot of people have to be its customers across the globe,' he says in his spacious fourth-floor cabin at Via's office in Bangalore's Manyata Business Park. 'The definition of service in India is very different and understanding those trends excited me that there is a large opportunity to build globally, not just in India.'

The venture started in a garage in Bangalore's Jayanagar area that the partners had rented for ₹6,200 a month and with seed capital of ₹15-20 lakh.

Gupta attributes Via's success and its journey to a 45,000-sq.ft swank office in a year and a half to the company's innovative practices and continuous efforts to be different.

The need to be innovative also emerged from wanting to stay ahead of the curve and a desire to offer customers more than the regular fare. 'Others offer transactional services, where a customer is given a helpline number that he calls in an emergency, but we offer personalized services. There is a personal travel assistant and a cell number given to you in the city you are traveling to, at no extra cost,' he says. 'Over a period of time, it makes a difference.'

The vision for Via has also been to create standardized, global products and services and take it to every neighbourhood. For example, under the 'Via bus tours' segment, the company arranges pilgrimages on luxury buses to destinations such as Tirupati, Vaishnodevi, Shirdi, and Puri. Recently, it launched a product—rail upgrade—that allows wait-listed railway passengers to get an upgrade and fly for as low as ₹499 over the train fare.

On a Saturday afternoon, when most offices, particularly in the information technology (IT) sector in Bangalore, are closed, the Via office is bustling with people. There are no fixed work hours for Gupta. On Sundays, he works half day. He usually spends the other half with his 10-year-old daughter Ragvi and wife Sarita.

Gupta, whose father was a senior official in the Bureau of Police Research and Development, himself travelled quite a bit in his younger days, living in Shimla, Delhi, Kolkata, and Pune. In 1999–2005, during his stay in the US, he worked with many companies on Wall Street, with his first stint being at Citigroup Inc. on its direct cash management systems team.

Gupta says entrepreneurship starts with the understanding that one is really committed to creating something. 'It's not about creating businesses, making money but taking some large problems and putting your passion, commitment behind them to create solutions for a large number of people, who will make you their first choice,' he says.

Although Via has raised money from investors, Gupta says the company generated cash flow within months of starting as travel agents made cash deposits before they booked with Via.

Growing at an annual pace of 30 per cent, Via is looking to raise more than $100 million from private equity funds to finance its growth and a global rollout. It plans to aggressively expand in West and South-East Asia. Via Philippines is already up, though Gupta is yet to visit the office. Via Indonesia has also been established and Gupta says that markets such as these are the locations the company is looking at.

'The keyword for us was to build a model that could be replicated in similar economies,' he says.

— ◆ —

Q&A
VINAY GUPTA

In a cluttered online travel market, what sets Via apart?
Our focus from the beginning is how we connect to the needs of the people, how we bring products to them that they can consume in a simple way. Via. com focuses on the needs of consumers and that's what sets us apart. When you buy from Via.com and you are in Srinagar and there is a curfew, we have 300 retailers who can help you. How do you preserve the travel agent, because people like the personalized services, while you productize the service without tampering with the price.

What prompted you to set up Via?
When I came back from the US, I had no clue that we are going to build this company. I used to read a lot of newspapers every morning and too much was happening in this space. What we realized was India being a cash economy, there are rich people in Meerut, Ludhiana, and Cochin. If you want to reach them and bring high-quality products, you can't just reach them through Via.com. Via.com also needs to have a channel that would communicate to them those services in the local language. We thought this is a model we can scale globally.

What are the challenges you have faced in your entrepreneurial journey?
When we first started talking to the travel industry itself, people said who are you? We did not know what IATA (the International Air Transport Association) was, what are airline relationships. We sat outside airlines offices for 6-8 hours every day for months together, just to get access to their inventory. We were coming up with a globally unique model and people couldn't relate to it. We had a new business model and hadn't fund-raised like others and didn't have capital at our disposal. And, of course, keeping the start-up pace and family together.

Where do you see the online travel business in India heading?

The online travel business in India is here to stay, and here to grow. Globally, the business is no longer about brands and market value. The business is about customer needs, products, platforms. People who will focus on closest-to-consumer needs will win.

As an entrepreneur, who are your role models?

My role model is Swami Vivekananda who used to say, 'Rise, awake'. You can learn from pretty much everyone around you. Learning has to be constant. Why a lot of people don't grow is because they are not willing to learn.

———— ❖ ————